Elizabeth Gaskell

Garland Reference Library of the Humanities (Vol. 50)

Elizabeth Gaskell
An Annotated Bibliography
1929-1975

Jeffrey Welch

Garland Publishing, Inc., New York & London

1977

Library of Congress Cataloging in Publication Data

Welch, Jeffrey.
    Elizabeth Gaskell : an annotated bibliography,
1929-1975.

    (Garland reference library of the humanities ; v. 50)
    Includes indexes.
    1. Gaskell, Elizabeth Cleghorn Stevenson, 1810-1865--
Bibliography.
Z8324.6.W44 [PR4711]016.823'8   75-42874
ISBN 0-8240-9950-8

Printed in the United States of America

For John

Contents

Preface

Elizabeth Cleghorn Stevenson Gaskell—"Lily" to her intimate friends, "Mrs. Gaskell" to traditional scholars, "Elizabeth Gaskell" to more recent critics—today receives increasing attention from scholars and critics interested in the fiction and social history of nineteenth-century Britain. This annotated bibliography provides a listing of critical and biographical works treating Elizabeth Gaskell that have been published since 1929. In that year two bibliographies were published: Clark S. Northup's comprehensive bibliographical supplement to Gerald DeWitt Sanders' *Elizabeth Gaskell* and Archie Stanton Whitfield's shorter bibliography appended to his *Mrs. Gaskell Her Life and Works*.

The present bibliography lists and annotates all articles, books, and dissertations on Elizabeth Gaskell, arranged according to year of publication, with entries listed alphabetically by author within each year. Reviews of important books follow the book entry and are given in order of publication. Continuing literary disputes are cross-referenced, and exchanges carried in the pages of a journal over a brief period of time are grouped as a single entry. While no attempt has been made to cite every passing reference to Elizabeth Gaskell or her work, all significant mentions have been included. The annotations give a cogent statement of the author's thesis and use, as far as possible, each author's own words.

Two appendices have been added. The first lists collected editions and editions of individual works published from 1929 to 1975. The second appendix provides a detailed chronology of Elizabeth Gaskell's life and the publication of her works.

A three-part index lists entries by author, by title of Gaskell works, and by subject.

I wish to thank the many people who assisted in the preparation of this bibliography, particularly Robert H. Super of the University of Michigan for his patient counsel during the early stages of research

PREFACE

and for his careful reading of an early version of the manuscript. He bears of course no responsibility for any errors in my work.

To Alice and Chester Shaver I owe thanks for their friendship and encouragement.

I am grateful to the University of Michigan Library, the Cleveland Public Library, the Oberlin College Library, and the Michigan State University Library for making available to me the valuable resources of their collections.

For their inspiring lectures and conversations about nineteenth-century literature I thank Jerome Hamilton Buckley and Robert Kiely of Harvard University, and Herbert Barrows of the University of Michigan.

Finally, I cannot sufficiently express my thanks to John Olmsted, now at Oberlin College, to whom this book is dedicated.

Key Abbreviations

EG   Elizabeth Cleghorn Gaskell
CB   Charlotte Brontë
HW   *Household Words*

Novels, Nouvelles, Short Stories

AR	*An Accursed Race* (1855)
C	*Cranford* (1853)
CC	*The Cage at Cranford* (1863)
CP	*Cousin Phillis, A Tale* (1864)
CSS	*Christmas Storms and Sunshine* (1848)
CT	*Curious if True* (1860)
DG	*The Doom of the Griffiths* (1858)
DNW	*A Dark Night's Work* (1863)
GW	*The Grey Woman* (1861)
HB	*The Half-Brothers* (1859)
HH	*Hand and Heart* (1849)
HJM	*The Heart of John Middleton* (1850)
HLA	*Half a Life-Time Ago* (1855)
LCB	*The Life of Charlotte Brontë* (1857)
LL	*Lizzie Leigh* (1850)
LMT	*Libbie Marsh's Three Eras* (1847)
LW	*Lois the Witch* (1859)
MB	*Mary Barton, A Tale of Manchester Life* (1848)
MC	*The Moorland Cottage* (1850)
MHC	*Mr. Harrison's Confessions* (1851)
MLL	*My Lady Ludlow* (1858)
MM	*The Manchester Marriage* (1860)
NS	*North and South* (1855)
ONS	*The Old Nurse's Story* (1852)

KEY ABBREVIATIONS

Elizabeth Gaskell

1929

1   Becker, May Lamberton. "The Reader's Guide," _Saturday_
       Review _of_ _Literature_ 31 Aug., 99.

       Mentions LCB in a short article on the subject of
    biography.

2   Devonshire, Marion Gladys. _The English Novel in France_
       _1830-1870._ London: University of London Press,
       Ltd, pp. 351-55.

       Lists reviews and dates of publication of MB, R, NS,
    C, LL, DNW, SL, CP, and WD from 1848-1870. EG "seems to
    have enjoyed a good reputation in France. Her social
    books were probably read more from a point of interest
    in English social history." For a more recent and more
    accurate treatment of this subject see 37.

3   Neff, Wanda Fraiken. _Victorian Working Women: An_
       Historical and Literary Study of Women in British
       Industries and Professions 1832-1850. New York:
       Columbia University Press. Pub. Doc. Diss.
       "Bibliography," pp. 276-83.

       Surveys 19th century attitudes to working women and
    investigates the particular conditions faced by the textile
    worker, the non-textile worker, the dressmaker, the
    governess and the idle woman. "To the Victorians belongs
    the discovery of the woman worker as an object of pity,
    and in the literature of the early nineteenth century one
    first finds her portrayed as a victim of long hours,
    unfavourable conditions, and general injustice, for whom
    something ought to be done."

       "Mrs. Gaskell, in her sympathetic and humorous
    pictures of the lives of the industrial poor, was the
    greatest force of her day. She made the homes real and
    the people in them. She educated her readers in matters
    new and strange. She explained what causes strikes, what
    Chartism meant, what misery entered the homes during periods
    of trade depression and disturbance. Her novels made clear
    the relation between such questions and the lives of working
    women. _North and South_ is easily the greatest novel of
    industrial life in English."

4   Payne, George Andrew. _Mrs. Gaskell: A Brief Biography._
       Manchester, England: Sherrat & Hughes.

Rev. in TLS 4 Dec. (1930), 1035.

A sketch of EG's life and works.

5 Sanders, Gerald DeWitt. Elizabeth Gaskell. With a
       Bibliography by Clark S. Northup. New Haven,
       Connecticut: Yale University Press [actually pub.
       Jan. 1930]. Cornell Studies in English XIV.
       "Bibliography," pp. 165-267.

           Rev. by R.F. Russell in London Mercury 22 (Jan. 1930),
       294; in TLS 4 Dec. (1930), 1035.

       This biographical-critical study of EG's longer works
   includes a chapter, one of the first on the subject, on
   EG's use of dialect. Northup's bibliography, which lists
   materials relating to EG under the headings, Bibliographies,
   Collective Editions, Undated Editions, and Biography and
   Criticism, is the most comprehensive to 1929. (See also
   6.)

       To the novel EG contributed both a new class of
   characters, "spinsters, doctors and servants," and a new
   perception of the circumstances of the life of the work-
   ingman. What made her contributions so lasting and
   effective was the "realistic" portrayal of such characters
   by the "correct representation of their conversations."

       In her career as a novelist EG gradually achieved a
   perfection of artistry culminating in WD. In earlier
   stories, MB, R, C, and NS, she dealt with character more
   effectively than plot. With NS, her "transition" novel,
   she left behind attempts to write a "novel with a purpose."
   While LCB consists mostly of CB's letters it puts EG "among
   the first of English biographers." An observable advance
   in "technique" is seen in SL. The structure of this novel
   reveals an "almost flawless skill in technique" which,
   combined with EG's powerful transformation of her historical
   material, makes SL "one of the great historical novels of
   the period." With WD EG became the "sheer novelist." The
   construction of this novel is almost "perfect." "Every
   phase in the development of the story is carefully prepared
   for; every happening, however simple, has some bearing
   upon character or plot development; every incident moves
   on to a seemingly inevitable result; and all is done so
   naturally that the reader is unaware of the carefully
   concealed technique." The earlier C "often too near
   pathos to be wholly humorous" cannot compare in artistry
   with WD, a novel "fit to rank with the best comedies in
   English fiction."

6 Whitfield, Archie Stanton. <u>Mrs</u> <u>Gaskell</u> <u>Her</u> <u>Life</u> <u>and</u> <u>Work</u>.
   London: George Routledge & Sons Ltd. Appendix II,
   pp. 219-20, compares the serial form and the revised
   form of <u>NS</u>. Appendix III, "A Bibliography of the
   Works of Elizabeth Cleghorn Gaskell and a listing
   of Biographical and Critical Notices," pp. 221-53.
   Reprinted by Folcroft Lib. Eds., 1973.

      Rev. by Gilbert Thomas in <u>Spectator</u> 6 July, 24; by
   Vita Sackville-West in <u>Nation</u> <u>&</u> <u>Atheneum</u> 45 (20 July),
   539; in <u>TLS</u> 25 July, 593.

      Provided in this biographical-critical study of EG's
   works is a bibliography that complements Northup's
   bibliography in 5.

      EG's special gift as a novelist is her "great analyt-
   ical understanding of the human heart." This sympathetic
   power "counterbalances her general lack of synthetic
   faculty," and remains the outstanding quality in her
   works. It is a power similar to but less sophisticated
   than that one finds in novelists like George Eliot and
   Thomas Hardy. Both <u>MB</u> and <u>NS</u> are "humanitarian" not
   political novels. <u>NS</u> is artistically superior because
   it is less melodramatic. EG's poor plotting in <u>C</u> is
   "atoned for by its spontaneity." In <u>R</u> EG first begins
   to display her fine power of psychological analysis. In
   this novel EG dared to "delineate passions" forbidden to
   novelists up to this time but because she herself could
   not transcend conventional attitudes of her age she drew
   a psychologically unconvincing portrait of the erring yet
   noble Ruth. A truly realistic handling of the "fallen
   woman" theme occurs in Hardy's <u>Tess</u>. CB's portrait in
   <u>LCB</u> is essentially accurate owing to EG's "presenting
   her characters objectively" through CB's "self-revealing"
   letters. EG's highest achievement is <u>SL</u>. By weaving
   together the historical material, the personal activities
   of her characters and in the manner of Hardy the influences of environment on human nature, she achieves a
   "unity of vision" which surpasses that in Thackeray's
   <u>Esmond</u>. Although her characters define themselves more
   by action than by thought EG made her "stand . . . between
   the naturalistic and the psychological novel, and gave
   us something approaching realism, life slightly idealized."
   <u>WD</u> proceeds in a mechanical "sequence" of scenes rather
   than as "an organic growth." Its characterizations of
   Molly Gibson and Cynthia Kirkpatrick are well drawn.
   EG displays great powers of sympathy in treating Mrs.
   Gibson.

1930

7 Haldane, Elizabeth Sanderson. Mrs. Gaskell And Her
       Friends. London: Hodder and Stoughton, Ltd.
       "Mrs. Gaskell's Writings," pp. 311-12.

       Rev. by Cecilia Townsend in Spectator 145 (22 Nov.),
   797; in TLS 4 Dec., 1035; in Week End Review 11 Dec., 1958;
   in Saturday Review of Literature 7 (11 July 1931), 963;
   (with other works) by Marjorie Nicolson in Yale Review
   NS 21 (Summer 1932), 852-55.

       This biography focuses attention on EG's relation-
   ships with CB, Florence Nightingale and Madame Mohl by
   introducing yet unpublished letters written by EG,
   principally, to the Winkworth sisters. Biographical
   information does not bear on the author's critical estimate of EG's works. As a writer EG did not find suitable
   material, nor did she prove herself a writer committed
   to genuine self-expression until she wrote C. "She had
   the real stuff in her that makes an original writer in-
   dependently of any outside urge" to achieve some social
   effect. C shows that she had a feminine observation but
   no deep psychological insight. In LCB she could not
   penetrate into the mental or emotional worlds of the
   Brontës. But her experience with the biography no doubt
   influenced her art, for in SL she attains "maturity" as
   a writer. In this story she blends the feminine observation of C with "elemental qualities" of character more
   in keeping with a wider world of thought and feeling.
   WD is EG's "best real novel" for C is not a novel. The
   subject of WD, "the people in a country town," was most
   congenial to her and in it she combines equally humor
   and "lessons to be taught."

8 Payne, George Andrew. "Charlotte Brontë's Biographer,"
       Brontë Society Transactions 7 no. 5 (part 40), 227-30.

       Address given to the Brontë Society 25 Jan. 1930 at
   its annual meeting at Bradford. Gives an account of EG's
   friendship with CB.

                            1931

9 Hopkins, A.B. "Liberalism in the Social Teachings of
       Mrs. Gaskell," The Social Service Review 5 (Mar.),
       57-73.

       "The liberal spirit as [EG] illustrates it means
   the application of Christian ethics to the immediate

                              6

problems of life, the actual trying out of Christian
principles--an age-old idea which is at the same time
new in that it has never been fully adopted, mauger
centuries of exhortation." Her discussion of "social
conditions" in her day in MB, NS, and R, and in the
rest of her works "is able but limited." Yet her
attitude to conflict, which always involved taking an
"imaginative grasp of the opposite point of view," is
not "old-fashioned" but rather suggestive and is, in
fact, coming into use by a "majority of present-day
thinkers and some capitalists."

10   Knight, Grant C. The Novel in English. New York:
          Richard R. Smith, Inc., p. 199 and passim.

          EG "always primly known as Mrs. Gaskell" is
remembered for MB, C and "an early psychological
novel" R.

11   Kooiman-Van Middendorp, Gerarda Maria, "Elizabeth
          Cleghorn Gaskell (1810-1865)," in The Hero in the
          Feminine Novel. Middleburg [and Amsterdam]: Firma
          G.W. Den Boer, pp. 82-95. Reprinted by
          Haskell House, 1966.

          "The spirit of the age required a character of a
nature different from the woman's ideal of more than
half a century before and Mrs. Gaskell . . . gratified
the general demand. Though all her heroes are men of
noble, generous characters, they do not manifest these
good qualities in the exaggerated manner of Richardson's
hero." "She let her heroes move in their own worlds
among people of their own rank and standing, and made
them speak in their own dialect and in their own way."
"She is the first novelist who introduced psychological
realism into the description of her hero's character
though her psychology did not go very deep."

1932

12   Brockbank, James. "Mrs. Gaskell and Silverdale," Papers
          of the Manchester Literary Club 57, 271-82.

          A short biographical essay pointing to the division
in EG's life between country and city. Silverdale in
North Lancashire, "the one spot 'beloved of all' and
written in her heart," is seen to be the pole in EG's
life opposite to Manchester.

13 Brown, W. Henry. "Mrs. Gaskell: A Manchester Influence,"
    Papers of the Manchester Literary Club 58, 13-26.

        Provides insights into the milieu of Manchester
    where EG settled, a bride, on her twenty-second birth-
    day, 29 Sept. 1832. The active life and exposure to new
    ideas in Manchester helped shape EG's sensibility as
    a novelist.

14 Cross, Wilbur L. The Development of the English Novel.
    New York: The Macmillan Company, pp. 180, 234-35,
    244.

        EG's principle contributions to the English novel
    are a sympathetic rendering of the "thoughts and wayward
    moods of children" and a new class of commonsensical
    characters comprised of nurses and housekeepers. She
    possessed a unique "style" of writing, one which "will
    never be imitated." In her reporting of social condi-
    tions she was more reliable than Dickens. Her great
    accomplishment is to be seen in R, one of the first
    "psychological novels." This novel "announces the
    approach of the psychological novel in a restricted
    sense. The outward sequence of its incidents is the
    correlative of an inner sequence of thought and feeling,
    which is brought into harmony with an ethical formula
    and accounted for in an analysis of motive." EG's concern
    in this novel is with the ethical doctrine of "the act
    and its train of good and evil" which stems from Carlyle
    and Comte. All of George Eliot's novels are "constructed
    on the ethical formula" of Mrs. Gaskell's R, but George
    Eliot fully accomplished what EG had done only in part.

15 Lovett, Robert Morss and Helen Sard Hughes. "Elizabeth
        Stevenson, Mrs. Gaskell (1810-1865)," in The History
        Of The Novel In England. Boston: Houghton Mifflin
        Company (The Riverside Press Cambridge), pp. 240-43.

        "A writer equally earnest [as Dickens] in employing
    the novel as an instrument of social change," EG looked
    to the upper classes for mitigation of class antagonism
    as did Kingsley and she wrote with knowledge of her
    subject. "She was thus a follower of Dickens in his
    humanitarian crusade, and also in his method. She wrote
    for Household Words, of which Dickens was editor, and
    necessarily adopted the latter's view that a novel should
    carry itself by dramatic narrative and scene, rather than
    by exposition and description." She found her material
    in the social movement, which she "understood" better
    than Dickens or Kingsley.

16   McLaughlin, Florence Catherine. "Mrs. Gaskell's
        Accomplishment as a Novelist in Her First Three
        Novels." Unpub. M.A. Thesis (University of
        Pittsburgh).

        Discusses MB, NS and R in order to cast light on
EG's weaknesses and strengths as a novelist. EG is
seen as a "transitional" figure harking back to the
eighteenth-century in matters of technique and style
but anticipating twentieth-century concerns with social
issues. The first three novels best reveal EG's strength,
her power to draw convincing servants, and her weaknesses, which result from her attempt to mount the
pulpit.

17   Schnurer, Clara. "Mrs. Gaskell's Fiction." Unpub.
        M.A. Thesis (University of Pennsylvania). "Appendix:
        A Note on The Life of Charlotte Brontë."

        A short, general, appreciative study which attempts
to show in EG's work "the development of an artistic
faculty . . . stimulated by early associations, by
intimate family relationships . . . [and] broadened by
friendship with intelligent men and women of her generation. It received sustenance, perhaps indirectly, from
a literary tradition. I have attempted further, to
estimate the vitality of her talent by consideration of
her themes, her use of setting, and her characterization."

18   Seccombe, Thomas. "Introduction" to Mary Barton.
        London: J.M. Dent & Sons Ltd.; New York: E.P.
        Dutton & Co. Inc., pp. vii-xiv. Everyman's Library,
        no. 598. "Complete List of Mrs. Gaskell's Works,"
        p. xiv. (See 240.)

        Standard biographical essay. Of all her works,
MB is "first, in colouring, dramatic effect, and vividness, as the result of transcript from real life, unsur-
passed by anything that she wrote during the whole of
her eighteen years of production."

19   Tuell, Anne Kimball. "Mrs. Gaskell," in A Victorian
        at Bay. Boston: Marshall Jones Company, Inc.,
        pp. 61-80.

        EG touches both the eighteenth and twentieth cen-
turies. Hers was an artistic temperament guided by a
naïve reading public and she wrote to please it by
adhering to convention in her stories. She is modern

in one respect--she had an "instinct for the significant
detail." She relied on this instinct rather than on
"deliberate effort," however, to achieve her best effects.
"She would be hurt to know herself classed to-day some-
what as an antiquarian novelist, a lover of the old and
the odd for the sake of age and oddity."

20   Whitehill, Jane, ed., and intro. Letters of Mrs. Gaskell
       and Charles Eliot Norton 1855-1865. London: Oxford
       University Press, pp. vii-xxix. Reprinted by
       Folcroft Lib. Eds., 1973.

       Rev. in TLS 6 Oct., 707; by E.F. Benson in Spectator
     149, 485; by Yvonne ffrench in London Mercury 27 Nov.,
     85-86; in Bookman (N.Y.) 75, 886; by T. Earle Welby in
     Bookman (London) 83, 210; in Saturday Review of Literature
     10 Dec., 304; in NYTBR 25 Dec., 9; in Oxford Magazine
     9 Feb. (1933), 410; by Samuel C. Chew in Yale Review NS
     22 (1933), 835-38; by T.S. Eliot in New England Quarterly
     6 (1933), 627-28; by Gerald Sanders in American Literature
     5 (1933), 192-93.

       The introduction provides biographical details
     about EG and Charles Eliot Norton and discusses the
     circumstances of their meeting in Rome and their subse-
     quent relationship.

                              1933

21   Anon. "The Gaskell Collection of Letters," Bulletin
       of the John Rylands Library Manchester 17, 193-94.

       Lists names of "noteworthy literary personalities"
     which appear in the library acquisition of "upwards of
     three hundred letters" for the Gaskell collection.

22   Becker, May Lamberton. "The Reader's Guide," Saturday
       Review of Literature 8 July, 697.

       In a letter published in this column, C is one of
     five titles recommended "for a young French student's
     introduction to modern English."

23   Parrish, Morris Longstreth. Victorian Lady Novelists:
       George Eliot, Mrs. Gaskell, The Brontë Sisters:
       First Editions in the Library at Dormy House, Pine
       Valley, New Jersey described with Notes. London:
       Constable and Company Limited, pp. 53-75. Reprinted
       by Franklin, 1969.

Rev. by John Carter in Publisher's Weekly 124, 1754-57.

Provides a list and bibliographical details of first editions of works by EG in the Parrish collection.

1934

24 Cunliffe, John W. "Mrs. Gaskell (1810-1865)," in Leaders of the Victorian Revolution. New York: D. Appleton-Century, Inc., pp. 113-15. Reprinted by Russell & Russell Inc., 1963.

A capsule biography focusing on EG's relationship with CB. "In spite of an occasional inclination for melodrama, Mrs. Gaskell's romance moves in a gentler sphere than that of the two Brontë sisters; she has genuine sympathy for the oppressed, but none of their fierce indignation and fiery passion."

25 Loveman, Amy. "The Clearing House," Saturday Review of Literature 17 Feb., 497.

Recommends C, among other titles, as reading matter for a thirteen year old girl living on a farm.

26 Masefield, Muriel. "The Life of Elizabeth Cleghorn Gaskell (1810-1865)," and "Mrs. Gaskell's Novels," in Women Novelists from Fanny Burney to George Eliot. London: Ivor Nicholson and Watson Ltd., pp. 161-72, 173-90. "Bibliography," p. 173. "Books about Mrs. Gaskell," p. 190. Reprinted by Books for Libraries Press, Inc. (Essay Index Reprint Series), 1967.

These two chapters (12 and 13) provide, respectively, general biographical information and plot summaries of the major works and a few short stories.

1935

27 Anon. "Memorabilia," N&Q 169, 379.

Mentions the Gaskell collection, in which are to be found many letters to Dickens, in the John Rylands Library.

28 Cecil, Lord David. "Mrs. Gaskell" in Early Victorian

Novelists: Essays in Revaluation. London:
Constable and Company Limited, pp. 207-50.
[Actually pub. Nov. 1934.]

The quality of EG's "femininity" plays a significant
part in her achievement as a novelist. Her restricted
life and restricted emotional range prevent her from
rendering convincing male characters and dramatic events.
In the sphere of "domestic fiction," however, hers is
a special artistry. She has a feminine gift of observation which gives her a "command of detail" and a "power
to divine a situation, to assess a character by the
slightest and most fleeting indication." She excells
in creating "two kinds of women whose lives are not
directly concerned with men." The first of these are
young girls, like Cynthia Kirkpatrick in WD, and the
second are spinster and servant types, "semi-comic
character parts in the regular English tradition."

She did not accomplish a wholly unblemished work
of art. The novel form and her social conscience
encouraged her to write "outside her range," and she
could not create convincing dramatic incidents. C, SL,
CP and WD make up her significant achievement. Of these
C is the "least faulty," for it takes the form "proper"
to EG's inspiration. Her best characters, Cynthia
Kirkpatrick and Mrs. Gibson, raise WD to "greater heights"
than C but WD is "too long" a book.

29 Delafield, E.M. [pseudonym for Edmée Elizabeth Monica
           De La Pasture] com., and intro. The Brontës:
           Their Lives Recorded by their Contemporaries.
           London: The Hogarth Press, pp. 13-20.

A compilation of extracts from EG's LCB supple-
mented by extracts from letters, reviews, reminiscences,
autobiographies and biographies of contemporaries. It
is the compiler's opinion that EG "suppressed, with more
skill than conscience, every aspect of Charlotte that
might have revealed her as a faulty human being, as well
as a high-minded sufferer."

30 Steuart, A. Francis. N&Q 169, 374.

The same story that inspired Tennyson's poem
"Rizpah" also is recalled in one of EG's novels as the
story "with the sad ending, 'The poor Rizpah.'"

31 Waller, Ross Douglas. "Articles by Mrs. Gaskell," TLS
           25 July, 477. For a similar announcement see Waller,

Bulletin of the John Rylands Library Manchester
20 (Jan. 1936), 25-27.

This letter announces the discovery of two articles
EG wrote and published in Sartain's Union Magazine (New
York and Philadelphia). The first of these, "'The Last
Generation in England.' By the author of 'Mary Barton.'
Communicated for Sartain's Union Magazine by Mary Howitt,"
5 (July 1849), 45-48, is an early sketch using material
which EG later incorporated in C. The second is,
"'Martha Preston,' By the author of 'Mary Barton,'"
6 (Feb. 1850), 133-8.

32 Waller, Ross Douglas, ed. "Letters Addressed to Mrs.
       Gaskell by Celebrated Contemporaries. Now in the
       Possession of The John Rylands Library." Bulletin
       of The John Rylands Library Manchester 19, 102-69.
       Reprinted by Manchester University Press and The
       Librarian, The John Rylands Library, 1935.

Describes and quotes from among the three hundred
letters recently deposited in the John Rylands Library
Gaskell collection. The letters are divided into four
categories: "Letters to E.C. and W. Gaskell, 2 vols.;
Miscellaneous Letters, 3 vols.; letters from W.S. Landor;
letters from Dickens."

1936

33 Britt, Albert. The Great Biographers. New York, London:
       Whittlesey House, McGraw-Hill Book Co. Inc., pp.
       125-27.

Compares EG's LCB to E.F. Benson's Charlotte Brontë,
London: Longmans, 1932. "To accept Mr. Benson's con-
clusions rather than those of Mrs. Gaskell is to conceive
of Charlotte Brontë as something near a genius instead
of a rather commonplace, mildly talented, hard working,
misunderstood, mistreated mid-Victorian lady." Had CB
to choose the biography "which most pleased her egotist
soul, it would be Benson's."

34 Utter, Robert Palfrey and Gwendolyn Bridges Needham.
       Pamela's Daughters. New York: The Macmillan
       Company, pp. 152, 346-47.

C: "Mrs. Gaskell furnished a whole village of old
maids, and old maids in very truth they are in every
word and thought and deed, but there is hardly a stock

trait in the whole village. There is a fineness of
texture in the drawing of these figures that Mary E.
Wilkins Freeman did not attain, and that Jane Austen did
not surpass. Cranford is the highwater mark of the old
maid in art."

MB: When the working-girl Mary Barton remonstrates
with Harry Carson she suggests Pamela "in her respect-
ful demeanor, but it is only a hint." The analysis
of Mary's discovery of "true love" is "real analysis
. . . of the mind and feelings of a real girl." The
phrase, "Now I can scorn you for plotting to ruin a poor
girl," may suggest the trite formula, but there is no
melodrama in it where we find it. Verbally, however,
it is a middle term between Pamela and Nellie the
Beautiful Cloak Model" (1906), a later Victorian "melodramatic novel."

1937

35   Baker, Ernest A. "Mrs. Gaskell and Other Women Novelists"
        in The History of the English Novel. 9 vols.
        London: H.F. & G. Witherby Ltd, 1924-1938, VIII,
        81-111.

MB, R, and NS are books in which EG's motives are
commendable but in which her "feelings overrode both
truth and logic." Incomparably more congenial to her
"true genius" is the subject matter of C, MLL and CP.
C is "happily perhaps . . . not a novel." "From first
to last, the writer is simply miniaturing still life,
and spinning indulgent comedy from the interplay and
byplay of quaint idiosyncracy in her little bevy of
womenfolk of the polite class." MHC gives many "fore-
tastes" of C, and MLL and CP are seen to be "nearest in
manner" to C. In SL EG "sins" by over-complicating her
plot with melodrama. In WD EG "built, if not better
than she knew, at least better than she intended." Her
three female characters in WD, Molly Gibson, Cynthia
Kirkpatrick and Mrs. Gibson, are well drawn. EG drew
"too directly from life," and she had a tendency to
"bring out the lesson . . . implied in a tale of wrong-
doing;" both these tendencies were encouraged at the
start by her sociological novels. As a result, she
could not keep "the calm, contemplative neutrality of
the artist."

36   Beard, Paul. "Introduction" to The Cage at Cranford,
        and Other Stories. London: Thomas Nelson & Sons,
        pp. 7-22. (See also 300, 315.)

(Not seen.)

1938

37   Hopkins, Annette B.   "Mrs. Gaskell in France 1849-1890,"
     PMLA 53, 545-74.   (See 2.)

     Provides tables showing editions and critical
reviews of EG's works published in France. She was
popular but no demonstrable influence of EG's can be
observed in the development of French literature in
the latter half of the century.

1939

38   Block, Andrew. The English Novel 1740-1850: A Catalogue
     Including Prose Romances, Short Stories, And
     Translations Of Foreign Fiction. With an Intro-
     duction by Ernest A. Baker. London: Grafton &
     Co., p. 85. New and revised edition with Intro-
     duction by John Crow, Dawsons of Pall Mall, 1961,
     p. 82.

     Provides transcriptions of title pages for EG's
works: LM, LL, MB, MC, SH, and CSS.

39   O'Clair, Robert M. "Mr. and Mrs. Victorian," Scholastic
     34 (6 May), 29-E.

     Mr. O'Clair's (age 16) essay derives inspiration
from Cecil's essays on EG and Anthony Trollope in 28.

1940

40   Anon. "Novels of the Week: Peace at Cranford," TLS
     10 Aug., 385.

     Notes publication of C, with wood engravings by
Joan Hassall. (See 263.) "A refined didactic essence
of Christian charity and good works distils its faintly
oppressive virtue into the air that Mrs. Gaskell
breathes, and the result is a degree of sentiment in
"Cranford," as in her solider and more ambitious
novels, that to-day is a little overpowering. Like
the profound emphasis of her sense of class distinctions,
such excess of conventionalized feeling is, indeed,
very much of the period. For even where the arts
of authorship were concerned, passion was denied to

genteel womankind, and since Mrs. Gaskell was neither
a Brontë nor an emancipated female like George Eliot,
the habit of an inveterate sentiment took its place."

41   Micklewright, Rev. F.H. Amphlett. "The Religion of Mrs.
        Gaskell," Modern Churchman June, 112-17.

        "The prophetic voices of F.D. Maurice and Mrs.
Gaskell awakened the soul of the English people at a
time when conventional dogmatic religion was powerless
to interfere in a life and death struggle."

                            1941

42   Pritchett, V.S. "Current Literature: Books in General,"
        New Statesman 21 June, 630. For a letter in
        response to this article objecting to Pritchett's
        statement that NS is out of print, see H.S. Milford,
        New Statesman 28 June, 652.

        An appreciation and defense of EG's "social novels,"
MB and NS, in response to Cecil's critical essay in 28.

        "All early and mid-Victorian fiction, with the
exception, perhaps, of Wuthering Heights, inculcates
the idea of responsibility, as our novels seem to
impress us with the ideas of self-sufficiency and guilt."
EG is in the mainstream of her time because her concerns
were those of her age and her early books reflect this.
"The truth is, I think, that a vital and brutal age,
intoxicated above all by the idea of power--not only
Carlyle, but Mrs. Gaskell too, had a weakness for the
rough Teutonic ancestor, the Viking and the Nordic myth--
could control itself only by moral violence." One might
not want to praise EG on these grounds, but one can
defend such books as NS and MB. "They were didactic
true to life stories in their time, and we must not
forget this when we find Cranford or the social comedy
of Wives and Daughters more to our taste."

        In NS as in all her work EG reveals her powers as
an observer with a "true eye and ear." NS itself "succeeds" where EG "always succeeds: in the essentials
of typical characters, in her skill at distinguishing
and presenting manners, in her delightful eye for
detail, the mild deftness of her satire." In the novel
she pits Margaret's pride against Thornton's obstinacy
and hard-headedness. The opposition and the battle
between the two is typical and true of the "northern
character" which has a "streak of sadism in it which

instinctively prefers enemies to friends." "This is
brought out even more successfully in the tale of
Thornton's relations with his workers. At first Margaret
sees only the mutual hatred in the relationship; then
she perceives that both sides like hating. It is a
sort of independence with them, a sport, an animal
instinct which on both sides, seeks not moral solutions,
but a master. The reconciliation of Thornton with the
strikè leader whom he has sacked and intends to victimise
is extraordinary but utterly truthful."

3 Roberts, Wright W. "English Autograph Letters In The
   John Rylands Library," Bulletin of the John
   Rylands Library Manchester 25, 119-36.

   This "general survey of correspondence" in the
library's collection mentions its Gaskell holdings.

1942

4 Bowen, Elizabeth. British Novelists. London: William
   Collins Sons and Company, Ltd., pp. 36-37.

   Of Charlotte and Emily Brontë, George Eliot and
EG, "in my heart I prefer Mrs. Gaskell--as sincere a
person, a less major artist and a more feminine soul."
"Her reaction to the injustices she found in industrial
England of that day was of the heart, but was ruled by
her steady head: unlike Dickens, she never overpainted;
truth seemed to her good, and bad, enough. She never
lost her love--and perhaps her nostalgia--for the sweet,
the comely, the orderly, the agreeable, though these,
to warrant her love, must be founded on moral right."
EG is remembered for C. When one reads Jane Austen's
Emma, then C, it becomes clear that in the forty years
between them England has changed. "Emma Woodhouse's
Highbury is unthreatened; Miss Matty's Cranford" is not
either but one can feel "vibrations from 'Drumble,' . . .
the not distant out-spreading Manchester."

5 Gerould, Gordon Hall. "The Victorian World in the Novel,"
   in The Patterns of English and American Fiction:
   A History. Boston: Little, Brown and Company,
   pp. 307-12.

   The "uneventful record" of EG's early life and
marriage "has importance only in that it shows her
opportunities for observing at close range a great
variety of people: employers and employed in the

industrial cities of the north, the rich and the poor
in the undisturbed countryside, Anglicans and Dissenters,
Londoners, and village dwellers of the most restricted
vision." But such experience had no immediate effect
on her artistry as a novelist. EG's early work "commands
respect" for its portraiture but its plot construction
is faulty. In SL she overcomes her problems of construction and in WD, her "masterpiece," "we are introduced to a widening group of persons so soundly imagined
and so perfectly integrated with their setting that we
are not likely to think of them as fictional. Without
apparent effort on the part of the author to deceive
us, the illusion of reality is nearly perfect." "No
single novel gives a better objective representation of
the Victorian world."

46   Grubb, Gerald Giles. "Dickens' Pattern of Weekly
        Serialization," ELH 9, 141-56.

        Examines "in a purely historical account" Dickens'
ideas and practice as an editor of serial publications.
EG's NS, published in Household Words, is seen as "one
of the most interesting examples of the shaping of a
story for serialization."

                          1943

47   Grubb, Gerald Giles. "Dickens' Editorial Methods,"
        Studies in Philology 40, 79-100.

        Complements 48, being a discussion of "editorial
methods developed in Dickens' guidance of his journals"
Household Words and All the Year Round "exclusive of
the subject of serialization." Dickens' careful attention to detail, the intensity and concentration of his
own working habits, and his tactful dealings with
writers in his employ account for his great success.
EG's is "an interesting case of a valuable contributor
made out of a highly individualistic writer, by a firm
but tactful editor." Represents EG as submitting to
Dickens' editorial methods after her conflicts with him
over NS.

        For a differing interpretation see 57.

48   Grubb, Gerald Giles. "The Editorial Policies of Charles
        Dickens," PMLA 58, 1110-24.

        Dickens adhered to editorial policies throughout his

career in journalism which assured his success as an
editor. His characteristic fair-mindedness brought him
to support EG in her clash with Dickens' publishers,
Bradbury and Evans, on the subject of advertising NS.
Nonetheless, EG herself could be determinedly independent
in a battle of wills. To insure that she get her way
with Bradbury and Evans she withheld the title of her
book until the publisher agreed to advertise it with
"sensible placards" and not with "hideous placards all
askew."

P., F. "The Good and the Clever," N&Q 185, 376.

EG, quoting in her LCB a passage written by Harriet
Martineau, completely overlooks Miss Martineau's misuse
of negatives. In a passage quoted by F.P., Alice
Meynell comments both on Miss Martineau's error and on
EG's missing it.

                        1944

Gilbert, Thomas. "Mrs Gaskell and George Eliot: A
      Study in Contrast," Chambers' Journal 121, 631-4.

Traditional ideas about these women writers, upon
re-examination, tend to be misleading. Characteristic
of EG, "this gentle Hellenic woman," is a fine balance
between "emotion and reason," which gave her a "truer
grasp of the social problems" of Manchester "than Dickens"
and prevented her from evading these problems, like
Disraeli, who "abandoned himself to theory and advocated
a benevolent autocracy." She wrote honestly yet she
could be "gay" in her honesty. But gaiety does not imply
a shallow character, for "far from being the personi-
fication of feminine charm at its gentlest," she "was
among the stoutest haters of complacency, the truest
rebels, of her day." In a novel like R, even though
"she allowed the spirit of the time to impose limitations
alien to her fundamental frankness," still the book was
"banned by libraries." Her only fault was that she
was too "generous;" she spent herself "too prodigally."
Her response to the social ills of her day--"Goodwill
is not enough: there must be careful, thorough understanding, not of abstract 'problems,' but of men by one
another"--"has no appearence of being out of date."

"If the elements in Mrs Gaskell were so fused that
her fine intellect has often received less than its
due, George Eliot, in whom intellect was more detached
and therefore more easily visible, has passed for being

more profound than her fellow-novelist." In fact, in
George Eliot one perceives a crippling duality: "an
intellectual craving for independence, an emotional
yearning for security." It led her to seek out and lean
on strong personalities; unfortunately, through George
Lewes, "a disciple of Comte," she became imbued with a
fashionable philosophy which failed to satisfy her whole
self. Like EG she was dissatisfied with the present
but unlike her she "had a nostalgic feeling for the past."
"For one whose imagination so tenderly cherished bygone
days, Positivism, which made so arbitrary a break with
the past, was far from being the best possible mental
stimulus." Superior as George Eliot is "artistically"
to EG, it is "Mrs Gaskell, besides entertaining and
charming us, [who] has still something to say which we
might heed." A "less bold and robust thinker" than EG,
"as a philosopher, George Eliot is sadly 'dated.'"

51 Lichfield, Dean of. "'Cold Loin' at Cranford," <u>TLS</u>
        15 Jan., 36.

    See responses by Sir Humphrey Milford, R.J.A.
Berry and Rev. George Andrew Payne in <u>TLS</u> 22 Jan., 48.

    The question is raised in this letter as to whether
"cold lion" not "cold loin" might be more appropriate
to describe the dish that Miss Matty served Miss Smith's
father when he visited Cranford (Ch. XIV, "Friends in
Need"). Readers are asked to examine editions earlier
than the 1891 <u>C</u>, with illustrations by Hugh Thomson,
to determine if "a compositor or publisher's reader of
normal gastronomical prejudices" did indeed alter the
spelling.

52 Wagenknecht, Edward Charles. "The Two Mrs. Gaskells,"
        in <u>Cavalcade</u> <u>of</u> <u>the</u> <u>English</u> <u>Novel</u>. New York: Henry
        Holt and Company, pp. 251-60. "Bibliography,"
        pp. 577-619. EG pp. 597-98. Reprinted by Henry
        Holt, 1954. "Bibliography and Supplementary
        Bibliography," pp. 577-660. EG pp. 597-98, 641.

    "In her novels, Mrs. Gaskell manifests an affinity
with the spirit of Dickens, but there is little or no
specific indebtedness to be shown." She was not "by
temperament a didactic writer." That is to say, the
"greater" EG was not didactic. It was the "lesser" EG
who wrote three "very important purpose-novels." The
"greater" EG wrote <u>C</u>, <u>SL</u> and <u>WD</u>. <u>WD</u> is her best novel,
a "very simple, though very long and perfectly constructed,
story."

1945

53 Grubb, Gerald Giles. "Dickens' Influence As An Editor,"
       Studies in Philology 42, 811-823.

       Summarizes the contents of 46, 47, 48, and suggests
    that "the integral whole" these articles form affords
    "at least a moment's realization of Dickens' significance
    in the field of popular magazine journalism." Also
    the article surveys the revival of periodical literature
    starting in the "early fifties of the last century"
    and Dickens' place in it.

54 Thomas, Gilbert. Builders and Makers: Occasional
       Studies. London: Epworth Press [actually pub.
       Dec. 1944].

       (Not seen.)

                          1946

55 Hinkley, Laura L. Ladies of Literature: Fanny Burney,
       Jane Austen, Charlotte and Emily Brontë, Elizabeth
       Barrett Browning, George Eliot. New York: Hastings
       House, Publishers, Inc.

       Mentions EG's relation to CB. CB's "best and, on
    the whole, most intimate of the friends . . . owed to
    her books" was EG. Both women would be surprised to
    learn that "her surest hold on posthumous fame--except
    perhaps Cranford--was to be that biography of her friend."

56 Hobman, Mrs. D.L. "Art or Life. A Woman's Problem,"
       Hibbert Journal 44, 258-62.

       The essential difficulty facing women who have
    artistic gifts finds its paradigm in the careers of CB
    and EG. For CB "it was the very intensity of her soli-
    tude which strengthened the wings of that imagination--
    less distraught than Emily's, more powerful than Anne's--
    enabling her to raise her limited experience to the
    heights of Olympus there to be transmuted into lasting
    works of art." Whereas, with a woman like EG, "it was
    out of the question [for her] to become completely
    absorbed in the development of her own gifts."

       "It is essentially a woman's problem, her time
    eroded by a thousand insistent claims which a man is
    usually spared." "Perhaps that is why so few women are
    to be found among the highest ranks of genius." If one
    seeks to answer such a question, the paucity cannot be

ascribed simply to poor education, lack of opportunity,
or mental inferiority. "But for most of them, as for
Mrs Gaskell, it is impossible to belong to themselves,
and like her they must be content only 'to have the
refuge of the hidden world of Art to shelter themselves
in.' Perhaps, after all, it was enough. It may be that
from the innumerable demands made upon her by life
her woman's nature ultimately derived its most lasting
and profound satisfaction."

57 Hopkins, Annette Brown. "Dickens and Mrs. Gaskell,"
        Huntington Library Quarterly 9, 357-85. (See 46,
        47, 48, 53 and 208.)

    Gives an account of the relationship between EG and
Dickens during publication of NS in HW, the alterations
in NS occasioned by serial publication, and analysis
of letters passed between EG and Dickens, Dickens and
his sub-editor, William Henry Wills, and Wills and
EG, during the 13 years EG wrote for Dickens.

    "The ultimate source of the trouble was that the
novel, by its very nature, was unsuitable for serialization on the Dickens pattern. The editor was mistaken
at the outset in his impulsive satisfaction over the
first batch of manuscript. A book in which a great deal
of the drama goes on in the minds of the characters does
not lend itself to mechanical divisions ending, with
every issue, on a strongly emotional note."

58 Malcolm-Hayes, Marian V. "Notes on the Gaskell Collection
        in the Central Library," Memoirs and Proceedings
        of the Manchester Literary & Philosophical Society
        87, 149-74.

    Glances at the Gaskell Collection in the Central
Library of Manchester, particularly at the subjects of
Biography and Criticism, Periodicals, and Works by the
Rev. William Gaskell, with a "hope to say something"
of Autographs and MSS.

59 Stebbins, Lucy Poate. "Elizabeth Gaskell," in A Victorian
        Album: Some Lady Novelists of the Period. New
        York: Columbia University Press, pp. 95-128.

    A biographical essay picturing EG as a woman
"unusually fortunate" in her placid life. Upbringing,
personal beauty and a prosperous life exempted her from
meeting the conditions needed to shape great artists.

"It was not necessary for her as it was for Charlotte
Brontë, to transform the fantastic images of her inner
life into fit shapes for public consumption, nor did she,
like George Eliot, need to remold painful forms. Life
was too kind to her as a woman to make her a great
artist."

1947

60 Anon. "Mrs. Gaskell's Manifesto," <u>TLS</u> 30 Aug., 438.

EG's plea in <u>MB</u> for "workers and masters to unite"
is quite opposite to the <u>Communist Manifesto</u>'s urging
the workers to "rise" against masters.   "The strife
of ideologies and the abracadabra of political economy
have led the world to a pretty pass; so, her simple
ideas have for many now a more alluring air of practi-
cality and common sense than the plans of the realists."
Although she was not comfortable in "the deeper probings
into the relations of men and the universe" she maintained
a sensible and honest view of the oppositions she observed in human life. She retreated eventually from
the "horrors of slavery and wealth" into the world of
Cranford and Hollingford of <u>WD</u>. "Unlike the Brontë
sisters, whose spell bound her so strongly, she presents
no dark anagrams of thought and mood to perplex our
searchings. Although she was unable to venture on peri-
lous seas of thought without danger of shipwreck, nor
into the deeper soundings of psychology, she was secure
in her casement of Cranford." "Even so, it is not difficult to find in the writings of this early-Victorian
lady hints of problems that are troubling the writers
of our own times."

61 Cooper, Lettice. "Introduction" to <u>Mary Barton</u>. London:
        John Lehmann Ltd, pp. v-xi. Chiltern Library,
        no. 6. (See 242.)

    Provides general background information on social,
historical and economic forces that shaped <u>MB</u>.

62 Harding, Robert. "Introduction" to <u>Cranford</u>. London:
        P. R. Gawthorn Ltd., pp. v-vi. The Russell Classics
        Series. (See 268.)

    A brief biographical essay.

63 Jenkins, Elizabeth. "Introduction" to <u>Cranford</u> [and]

Cousin Phillis. London: John Lehmann Ltd, pp.
v-xiii. (See 267, 302.)

(Not seen.)

64 Lane, Margaret. "Introduction" to The Life of Charlotte
    Brontë. London: John Lehmann Ltd, pp. v-xiii.
    The Chiltern Library, no. 12. Reprinted as
    "Mrs. Gaskell's Task," in Lane, Purely for Pleasure.
    New York: Alfred A. Knopf, 1967. (See 291.)

    Despite its shortcomings, LCB "is still in essence
    'truer' than anything about the Brontës which has been
    written since." EG "suppressed the truth somewhat"
    about CB's passion for M. Heger. "To have hinted at
    Charlotte's plight would have been a betrayal," if we
    consider the Victorian ideal conception of woman both
    CB and EG shared.

65 Lehmann, Rosamund. "A Neglected Victorian Classic,"
    Penguin New Writing no. 32, 89-101. Reprinted
    as "Introduction" to Wives and Daughters. London:
    John Lehmann Ltd, 1948, pp. 5-15. (See 304.)

    An "intensely feminine" author, EG's last novel
    "reflects in placid luminosity the wholeness of a dis-
    tinguished nature." Cecil, 28, errs in suggesting that
    she could not draw male characters; although, at times
    in WD, she does fall back on drawing "stock" characters.
    The book "will live" on account of its three major
    female portraits, Molly Gibson, Mrs. Gibson and Cynthia
    Kirkpatrick. Of the three Cynthia is unique in EG's
    works.

                          1948

66 Anon. "Anniversaries: An Exhibition of Books Published
    in 1648, 1748, 1848," Bulletin of the New York
    Public Library 52, 289-99.

    Exhibition of materials from the Henry W. and
    Albert A. Berg Collection, including a first edition
    of MB.

67 C., T. [Coolidge, T.] "Library Notes: Mrs. Gaskell to
    Ruskin," More Books [The Bulletin of the Boston
    Public Library] 23 no. 6, 229-30.

                          24

Prints two hitherto unpublished letters by EG, the
first to Geraldine Jewsbury (2 Apr. 1849) and the second
to Ruskin (Feb. 1865).

8 Curl, Joan, "Cranford Revisited," The Geographical
       Magazine May, 4-7.

Brief article with photographs and descriptions of
Knutsford buildings and practices familiar to lovers
of C.

9 Hopkins, Annette B. "Mary Barton: A Victorian Best
       Seller," Trollopian 3, 1-18.

Despite its weaknesses and some abusive criticism
at its appearance, MB brought EG immediate fame and
favorable commendations from "some of [her] most dis-
tinguished contemporaries."

In MB EG "is trustworthy" when portraying the social
conditions of the working class. The book does suffer,
in part, from the narrative shift of attention to Mary
Barton in its second half, and from its "denouement,"
which "modern critics" call "sentimental." However,
"in the light of instances of forgiveness accorded to
enemies that have been reported during the last world
war, the reconciliation between Carson and Barton can
hardly be said to falsify human conduct."

10 Lewis, Naomi. "Books in General," New Statesman 10 July,
       33. Reprinted as "Mrs. Gaskell," in Lewis, A
       Visit to Mrs. Wilcox. London: The Cresset Press,
       1957, pp. 167-74.

An appreciation of EG inspired by publication of
editions of MB, LCB, C [and] CP, and WD, by John Lehmann
Ltd.

One finds in EG's work the paradox of "the placid
garden and the Manchester slum" existing side by side,
for EG was brought in the course of her life to become
intimately acquainted with both worlds. But EG's "most
individual gift was for comedy" and C, "written in
separate sketches . . . has the episodic form that best
suited her."

"For a writer of her quality, Mrs. Gaskell had
curiously little critical sense, and even less literary
vanity. If she did not realize her weaknesses, she

really did not know how well, at times, she was writing."
"But it is in plot that an age asserts itself in its
novels, and when Mrs. Gaskell forces her characters into
refined and lingering illnesses, sudden voyages, marriages
and deaths which they seem mutely to resist, then, only
for a moment we remember the Victorian lady for whom
writing was a refuge and not her sole occupation."

71   Marchand, Leslie A.   "The Symington Collection," Journal
     of the Rutgers University Library 12, 1-15. (See 75.)

     Refers both to manuscript letters to and from EG
and to C.K. Shorter's notes for a biography of EG.

72   Raymond, Ernest.   In the Steps of the Brontës.   London:
     Rich and Cowan.

     Mentions EG's attitudes towards various Brontë
family members and gives a very short account of indis-
cretions in LCB.

73   Sholto-Douglas, Nora I.   Synopses of English Fiction.
     New York: Frederick A. Stokes Company Publishers.

     The book is divided into two parts.   Part I (1557-1810:
synopses 1-38) "traces the gradual transition of the
novel from the pure romance, depending for its interest
solely on incident, and that of a more or less improbable
nature, to the more modern conception of the novel,
where the chief interest hangs on character-development
and analysis of motive.   Part II (after 1810: synopses
39-75) "deals with a selection of novels of literary
merit which are not as well known to the general public
as they deserve to be."   Each synopsis is followed by
a "short critique calculated to show the relative value
of each novel treated."   Synopses given of no. 69 MB,
pp. 344-48, and no. 70 NS, pp. 348-51.

                              1949

74   ffrench, Yvonne.   Mrs. Gaskell.   London: Home & Van
     Thal; Denver: Alan Swallow.   The English Novelists
     Series.   "Bibliography," p. 108.   "Works by Mrs.
     Gaskell," p. 110.

     Rev. by Robert Halsband in Saturday Review of
Literature 29 Apr., 38,; by C.E. Vulliamy in Spectator
182, 614, 616; in TLS 13 May, 310; in N&Q 194, 308; by

Naomi Lewis in New Statesman NS 38, 128-29; (with other
works) in Nineteenth Century Fiction 5 (1950), 81-82.

Despite the fact that "there is nothing spectacular
about her work or personality" EG had a strong and per-
vasive sympathetic "understanding" and her best work
reveals "virtues" rarely matched in other novelists.
Until NS her work is of negligible interest. In NS
she reveals an increasing interest in "human relationships." This interest found a worthy focus in CB,
whose life appealed to that part of EG that sought to
"relive" lives capable of greater violence than her own.
MLL shows a growing maturity. It is in most respects
superior to C. C "immortalized the parochial scene;"
MLL "ennobled the village." Of greater consequence than
MLL is SL. This work shows the impact of the composition
of LCB, which urged EG "unconsciously" to attempt a grander
and more fierce story. EG shows her mastery of plotting
a story in CP but it is in WD that she breaks "free
from religious interest" in her construction of a
"straightforward love story." "Its construction is
splendid, and her interplay of action and development
worked out with a precision that places it technically
in the front rank with the masterpieces of domestic
fiction."

5 Marchand, Leslie A. "An Addition to the Census of Brontë
        Manuscripts," Nineteenth Century Fiction 4, 81-84.
        (See 71.)

In the private library of J. Alex Symington, recently
acquired by the Rutgers University Library, one finds
among other things Gaskell family correspondence,
including 2 letters of EG to J.S. Mill "and a penciled
draft of his reply to the first one." The subject is
a passage quoted in LCB in a "letter of Charlotte Brontë
criticizing the author of an anonymous article." The
author of the article on "The Emancipation of Women" in
Westminster Review was Harriet Taylor, later Mrs. Mill.

                         1950

6 Anon. "Charlotte Brontë and Harriet Martineau," TLS
        9 June, 364.

Harriet Martineau's marginalia in her edition of
LCB show that she "had only trifling charges to make
against the biographer" for the way she had been presented.
Examination of the passages in LCB "to which exception was
taken from one side or another suggests that many were

quotations from Charlotte's letters and that information
contained in others could only have been obtained from
[Harriet Martineau herself]."

77   Bland, D.S.   "Mary Barton and Historical Accuracy,"
        Review of English Studies NS 1, 58-60.

        In MB the opening scene in Green Heys Fields sug-
gests that holidays for workingmen were an institution
and that open areas for recreation were accessible to
the working-classes in 1839-40. Evidence contradicting
EG is cited in a report written by Dr. J.P. Kay (later
Sir James Kay-Shuttleworth) in 1833. "Faced with this
discrepancy, then, it is gratifying to be able to report
that Mrs. Gaskell can be justified at the expense of
the more scientific Dr. Kay, and that the value of
literary evidence to the social historian who is concerned with what Dr. Eileen Power once called 'reaching
beyond accuracy to truth' can, in this case at least,
be shown to be considerable." The scene in Green Heys
Fields is shown to be not only historically accurate
but also thematically important to the "emotional values"
of the novel.

78   Boggs, Arthur W.   "Reflections of Unitarianism in Mrs.
        Gaskell's Novels." Unpub. Doc. Diss. (University
        of California, Berkeley).

        Attempts to determine whether EG reflects "signifi-
cant principles of Unitarianism" in her "ten novels:"
MB, R, NS, SL, WD, MC, MLL, DNW, and CP. It is determined that certain tenets of Unitarianism, for example
that "man was kindly, benevolent, and basically good,"
are always present in her stories. R is "the most
Unitarian of her novels" because it illustrates almost
every Unitarian ideal. After C and MLL EG became more
adept at portraying "good characters;" by emphasizing
their peculiar foibles she was able to give them a more
pronounced individuality.

79   Hopkins, Annette Brown.   "A Uniquely Illustrated
        'Cranford'," Nineteenth Century Fiction 4, 299-
        314. (See 92.)

        A unique edition of C illustrated by William Henry
Drake, in the possession of the Huntington Library, is
shown to have illustrations traced from Hugh Thomson's
illustrations in EG's C, Macmillan, 1898.

0   Rubenius, Aina. The Woman Question in Mrs. Gaskell's
        Life and Works. Upsala: A.-B. Lundequistska
        Bokhandeln. Cambridge, Massachusetts: Harvard
        University Press, 1951. Essays and Studies on
        English Language and Literature. Edited by S.B.
        Liljegren, no. 5. "Appendix I: Factory Work for
        Women," pp. 232-40, provides historical material.
        "Appendix II: Literary Influences in Mrs. Gaskell's
        Works," pp. 241-83, examines "unconscious plagiarism"
        in EG's works. "Appendix III: Mrs. Gaskell's
        Quotations from and References to Other Writers and
        Works," pp. 284-370, "Mrs. Gaskell's Works with
        Dates of First Appearance," pp. 371-72. "Biblio-
        graphy," pp. 373-86.

        Rev. by Andrew Hilen in Studia Neophilologica 24,
    218-20; by Annette Brown Hopkins in Trollopian 7, 140-42.

        Examines EG's "attitudes towards problems of
    special importance to women," as they are revealed both
    through an analysis of the problems which faced EG her-
    self and then as they are seen to be reflected in her
    works.

        EG's married life was not placid and unstrained.
    Her own consciousness of the "woman question" was not
    only particularly acute, but also she had numerous
    female friends equally interested in the subject. In
    her own life she faced the conflict between obligations
    to her family and to her creative literary impulse. She
    never treated this conflict in her books, perhaps because
    she herself could not resolve it satisfactorily. But
    one can see a progression in her early stories from
    portraits of "passive" wives to "active" ones who are
    willing to defy their husbands if the opposition springs
    from an aroused maternal instinct. This change in her
    stories is seen to coincide with a change in her own
    feeling about a wife's role in the marriage relation
    between 1851 and 1858. Unfortunately EG did not use her
    works to try to reform the various social institutions
    which influenced the working woman.

                            1951

31 Bowen, Elizabeth. "Introduction" to North and South.
        London: John Lehmann Ltd, pp. v-viii. The Chiltern
        Library, no. 21. Reprinted in Bowen, Seven Winters
        Memories of a Dublin Childhood & Afterthoughts Pieces on
        Writing. New York: Alfred A. Knopf, pp. 139-47.

        NS is a "drama, a novel based upon contrasts conflicts

and oppositions." It takes in, in the widest possible
way, the study of oppositions having a "psychic significance that cuts down deep in many of us." The book
should be read not primarily as a "social document,"
although it is that, but as a work of "feeling." "It
was not . . . Mrs. Gaskell's purpose to write yet
another love story boned on pride and prejudice. Margaret
Hale and John Thornton play their parts as embodiments
of the wider forces contending in North and South." "But,
while one would insult Mrs. Gaskell were one to ignore
or dismiss her moral aims . . . to us North and South
must appeal on other grounds--as a novel of manners,
a precise and peculiarly fearless study of class
feeling, and a work of what is from time to time an
almost voluptuous sensibility."

82   Sadleir, Michael. XIX Century Fiction: A Bibliographical
     Record Based On His Own Collection By Michael
     Sadleir. Cambridge, England: Cambridge University
     Press, I, 378. 2 vols. Reprinted by
     Cooper Square Publishers, Inc., 1969. 2 vols.

     Provides a list of EG's principal fiction, in order
     of rarity.

83   Thirkell, Angela. "Introduction" to Cranford. London:
     Hamish Hamilton Ltd., pp. v-xxxi. (See 272.)

     (Not seen.)

                          1952

84   Ascoli, David. "Introduction" to Cranford. London:
     William Collins Sons, pp. 9-14. (See 274.)

     (Not seen.)

85   Hopkins, Annette Brown. Elizabeth Gaskell: Her Life
     and Works. London: John Lehmann Ltd. "Appendix:
     Bibliography," pp. 333-40, includes: books by EG
     "listed in the order of their first publication;"
     "contributions to magazines, listed in chronological
     order;" "collections of stories;" "collected works;"
     "prefaces to and articles by Mrs. Gaskell in books
     by other writers," and "earlier biographical
     studies of Mrs. Gaskell." "Bibliographical Notes
     and Illustrative Material," pp. 341-76.

Rev. by Margaret Lane in New Statesman 32, 323;
by David Cecil in Listener 47, 483; by Naomi Lewis in
Observer 23 Mar., 7; in TLS 28 Mar., 220; by J. Squire
in Illus. London News 220, 702; by T. Hill in Dickensian
48, 175-76; by Sylvia Norman in Fortnightly Review 171,
355-56; by Phyllis Bentley in Brontë Society Transactions
12 no. 2 (part 62), 119-20; by Paul Le Moal in Études
Anglaises 6, 60-61.

Old myths in EG's life are examined and corrected
in this the only full length biography of EG. For
example, the manuscript of MB did not go the round of
London publishers but rather "seems to have been accepted
by the first firm to whom it was offered." MB, EG's
first novel, was not produced by a too feeling, uninformed
Victorian lady but rather by a mature, unsentimental
and acutely observant woman. EG had already exhibited
a propensity for writing, well before her boy William
died of scarlet fever. And, while her early work reveals
a woman genuinely concerned "for the lot of the humble
people about her . . . and bears the imprint of deep
sorrow," the maturity of her thought and feeling was
already determined, as the portrait by George Richmond,
made sometime in 1851, testifies.

MB: This was the first industrial novel "to combine
sincerity of purpose, convincing portrayal of character,
and a largely unprejudiced picture of certain aspects
of industrial life." EG successfully weaves the tragic
story of John Barton with Mary Barton's romantic one,
despite the shift of emphasis required when the publisher
wished to change the title from "John" to "Mary Barton."
The reconciliation scene is not improbable, given the
behavior of people during the second world war, nor is
the ending "sentimental," for EG refrains from giving
any kind of easy solution to the social conflicts presented
in her story.

C: The fact that C is "practically structureless
. . . contributes to its charm." It is united by "mood,"
"spirit" and "tone." The fictional world of C was close
to EG's heart and her story CC shows how easily she could
recapture its "tone." C reveals EG's "passion for the
country, that came out again and again" in the stories
of this woman bound to live in Manchester.

R: Though lacking complete artistry, this novel
rises high above "the level of pure propaganda" owing
to "character drawing, its descriptive power, the clear
presentation of the problem, and the reasonableness with
which it is handled." In R she introduced two new
elements into the treatment of the "fallen woman" theme:

the illegitimate child contributes to its mother's salvation, not shame; she suggests that marriage is not
"expedient" as "a way to social salvation."

NS: A highlight of the biography is the discussion
of the serial publication of the novel in HW. See also
57. In NS her interest is not predominately the industrial theme but "moulding her characters." The industrial theme is useful, however, for introducing her
characters, which she draws with a psychological truth-
fulness and embeds in a believable milieu.

LCB: The portrait of CB is "always sympathetic but
not uncritical."

Letters: Correspondence with George Smith, begun
when she was writing LCB, reveals the professional
literary woman. Letters to Charles Eliot Norton, with
whom she became closely acquainted in 1857 in Rome,
show the "social" woman.

MLL: The short stories written between 1857 and
1863 are uneven in quality, partly because EG wrote many
of them for money. MLL, the best of them, is ruined by
the story within a story.

SL and CP: In these stores, EG reached a high
quality of art. "Structural defects" injure SL her
"historical novel;" what we do admire, however, are the
"vivid beauty of the country scenes," and "the convincing
truth with which the characters are portrayed." Shorter
than SL, CP is an almost "flawless" tale in which EG's
descriptive powers are at their best. The stance of
the narrator, Paul Manning, weakens the story because
it is improbable that he can be near Phillis but not be
in any sense in love with her.

WD: This "crowning effort" of her achievement brings
EG close to the stature of Jane Austen, for EG submerged
perfectly her moral concerns in her narrative. In this
novel we find her finest characters, Cynthia Kirkpatrick
and Mrs. Gibson.

In Retrospect: Among women novelists EG merits high
regard. Her humor "can bear comparison with Jane Austen."
In her concern with psychological states she "touches"
the Brontës. She is superior to George Eliot in dealing
with the doctrine of the act and its train of consequences,
because she wrote transcriptions from life. George Eliot's
knowledge, which came from "passionate reading," was
largely theoretical in nature.

86 Lane, Margaret. "The Hazards of Biography: Mrs. Gaskell
      and Charlotte Brontë." Illustrations by Joan
      Hassall. Cornhill Magazine 166, 154-79.

      An abridgement, in which some paragraphs are
slightly rearranged, of 91.

87 Lehmann, Rosamund. "Three Giants: Charlotte Brontë,
      Mrs. Gaskell and George Eliot," New York Times
      Book Review 21 Dec., 5.

      "Three giants they were, emerging at roughly
the same historical moment in the century: the middle
period--the most vital and productive both culturally
and materially. They emerged along with such giants as
Dickens, Thackeray, Carlyle--not only emerged but took
their places beside them. It was an era of prosperity
for the male giant; but, for the first time in our
literary history, women began to claim and earn the
right to equal them in stature."

                          1953

88 Anon. "Two Letters From Charlotte Brontë to Mrs.
      Gaskell," Brontë Society Transactions NS 12 no.
      2 (Part 62), 121-23.

      Reprints two letters published in 85. The originals
of these letters are in the Arts Library of the University
of Manchester.

89 Bourret, Jeanne. "Elisabeth Gaskell, écrivain intimiste,"
      Revue Générale Belge(Brussels) Sept., 788-94.

      (Not seen.)

90 Collins, H.P. "The Naked Sensibility: Mrs. Gaskell,"
      Essays in Criticism 3, 60-72.

      Inquires into the relationship between EG's religious
views and the character of her novelist's sensibility.
"It is impossible not to feel that Elizabeth, for all
her exaggerated reserve and decorum, had a religious
hunger of a kind that would have been incomprehensible
to a Priestley or a Martineau. Her natural piety was
not the passive piety she showed. Did Unitarianism
really touch her religious sense? Or is it not rather
true that 'religion' held her mind at something under

                          33

adult level?" EG only began to transcend a "nursery
school" morality in her later work, and one can observe
the correspondence between a rather simple religious
emotion--"she had no ecstacy"--and a "naked sensibility"
which openly testifies to the "simple impact of life upon
her." "She had no real defences, no real artifice, and
in literary creation, which 'disrealizes and realizes,
realizes and disrealizes' she is ultimately ingenuous."

"The supremely good things, surely, are her sensi-
tiveness, sympathy with human nature, humour, playful-
ness, and insight into not-too-complex character, above
all acute feeling for the beauty of the English scene
at its best. But her vision of life was confined within
her own _instinctive_ feminine sympathies; she never
created an objective, dramatized world in which men and
women live without realizing the lineaments of their
creator."

91 Lane, Margaret. The Brontë Story: A Reconsideration
    of Mrs. Gaskell's Life of Charlotte Brontë.
    Illustrated by Joan Hassall. London: William
    Heinemann Ltd.

    Since this book is intended for "the general reader"
the "aim . . . has been to place the reader in a discreet
position behind Mrs. Gaskell's shoulder, where he can
comfortably see what she is writing, and watch her
tackle her difficulties as she encounters them; and
while he is thus strategically placed, to put into
his hand all the material to which Mrs. Gaskell had no
access, or which, for one good reason or another, she
did not use; so he will, by the time he sees her come
to her last page, be able to fill in all the gaps and
make his own deductions and interpretations."

92 Lauterbach, Edward S. "A Note on 'A Uniquely Illustrated
    Cranford'," Nineteenth Century Fiction 8, 232-34.

    Pounts out errors in 79, but affirms that Hopkins
"is probably right in deducing that [W.H.] Drake traced
the illustrations from Hugh Thomson's pen-and-ink drawings
in _Cranford_, Macmillan, 1891."

93 Raymond, Ernest. "The Brontë Legend, Its Cause and
    Treatment," Essays by Divers Hands 26, 127-41.
    The essay was read 24 Nov. 1948.

    The lecture examines the evidence and character of

several victims of the Brontë "Legend" such as Mr. Brontë,
Aunt Branwell and M. and Mme Heger.

94   Thompson, Laurence Victor, ed. Blue Plaque Guide To
         Historic London Houses And The Lives Of Their
         Famous Residents. London: Newman Neame, pp. 44-45.

     (Not seen.)

                              1954

95   Allen, Walter. The English Novel: A Short Critical
         History. New York: E.P. Dutton & Co., Inc.,
         pp. 208-14.

         EG as a writer is "not quite easy to judge" because
     her "most successful works" C and WD probably would not
     today insure her "claim to importance as a novelist."
     "It was, in a sense, a virtue in Mrs. Gaskell that she
     did not know her place as a novelist, and very imper-
     fect as Mary Barton (1848) and North and South (1855)
     are, it is on these novels that her reputation rests."

         NS is a "much better" book that MB because it
     "remained much more closely in its author's range of
     talent," and because EG's social analysis is acute and
     convincing. "In no other Victorian novel does one get
     the sense so strongly of England as two nations, not
     Disraeli's two nations of rich and poor, but the two
     nations of the agricultural, feudal, Trollopean South
     and the industrial North." Because we see the North
     from the "outside," that is from Margaret Hale's point
     of view, "we discover the North as Margaret Hale dis-
     covers it." We find in John Thornton, the Milton mill-
     owner in NS, EG's "most successful male character."
     "He is not a dream figure; he has been observed by a
     woman who knows the world and is judged in the novel
     by a girl of high spirits, intelligence, and assured
     values."

96   Hopkins, Annette Brown. "A Letter of Advice from the
         Author of Cranford to an Aspiring Novelist,"
         Princeton University Library Chronicle 15, 142-50.
         The letter is reprinted as "A Letter of Advice,"
         in London Magazine 1, 73-75.

         In this letter, written to a woman she did not know,
     EG urges the woman to achieve perfection as a wife,
     mother and housekeeper before embarking on a novelist's
     career.

97 LeClaire, Lucien. A General Analytical Bibliography of
    the Regional Novelists of the British Isles
    1800-1950. Clermont-Ferrand, France: G. DeBussac,
    pp. 87-93.

    "This analytical bibliography aims at presenting
    a convenient and expressive table of novelists over the
    period 1800-1950, with, for each of them, a few bio-
    graphical notes, the titles of the novels of interest
    in the regional connexion, their various editions so
    far as could be ascertained, and whenever possible, the
    scene of each novel."

    In the short introductory paragraph to Ch. 2 "The
    Novel Becomes Localized 'Into the Bargain' 1830-1870,"
    pp. 51-119, it is noted that during the years 1830-1870
    novelists tended to specialize in a region, owing partly
    to the influence of realism as a style and partly to
    accident of birth and residence. An unconscious or half-
    subconscious desire to develop and present the "whole
    colouring" and "mental atmosphere" of a region or
    locality begins to predominate in the English novel.
    Yet one does not find a unified "technique" for the
    regional novel in this period.

98 Swinnerton, Frank. "Introduction" to Cranford. London:
    J.M. Dent & Sons Ltd.; New York: E.P. Dutton &
    Co. Inc., pp. vi-xii. [actually pub. 20 Jan. 1955.]
    "Select Bibliography," p. xiii. (See 276.)

    C is EG's "unique" and enduring achievement.

99 Tillotson, Kathleen. "Mary Barton," in Novels of the
    Eighteen-Forties. Oxford: Clarendon Press, pp.
    202-23.

    Rev. by Pansy Packenham in Dickensian 50, 186-87;
    by John Butt in Durham University Journal 47, 40-42;
    Arundell Esdaille in English 10, 109-10; in N&Q NS 1
    [199], 552; by V.S. Pritchett in New Statesman 17 July,
    78-79; by Rex Warner in Spectator 2 July, 24-26; in TLS
    23 July, 472.

    MB is the "outstanding example" of a kind of novel
    "which first clearly disengaged itself in the forties:
    the novel directly concerned with a social problem, and
    especially with the 'condition-of-England question.'"
    Yet, it is not simply a "social novel." "A wider impar-
    tiality, a tenderer humanity, and it may be a greater
    artistic integrity, raise this novel beyond the conditions

and problems that give rise to it."

EG's great asset is her power of feminine compassion
realized in characterization. In contrast Disraeli's
Sybil loses much potential power because it lacks "a
character in whom we are asked to take any human interest." EG's sympathy reaches deep into John Barton's
nature to show how he responds not only to the simple
wrongness of poor living conditions for workers but
also to the "hard core of irremediable suffering 'permanent, obscure, and dark' in his sense of the mysterious
injustice of man's time bound existence. To counteract
this there must also be a reconciling power; the sense
that 'we have all of us one human heart.'"

The novel has a "complex unity" not governed by
its "social purpose" but by "theme and tone." It also
has a unity deriving from its central character, John
Barton. He affects both the "mere narrative" and the
"theme of class antagonism" because both reach their
climax in Ch. 18 "Murder," the center of the book. Yet
he is "bigger than the events," for he is the "timeless
history of how a man full of human kindness is hardened
into (and by) hatred and violence." Through this character EG examines the silent suffering human soul.

The change of title from "John" to "Mary Barton"
gave the novel, perhaps, a more "marketable" title,
but John Barton bears the burden of the story. Mary
Barton draws "importance from the story," John Barton
"gives out strength to it."

To counter the growing despair of John Barton EG
provides, in Job Legh, a spokesman for "the gentle
humanities of earth," those values that must be urged
in the face of bitterness and the "frustrations of
political action." EG "holds the balance" between the
two characters to prevent a too easy or complacent judgment. She does not confuse "resignation to the power
of the masters and the divine will." "The lesson that
Job Legh presses home is that of John Barton's terrible
act, without which Mr. Carson's eyes could not have
been opened, and for which the masters must share the
responsibility."

EG's contribution to the novel stems from her
courage and sympathy and from her "quiet assumption
that to know is to understand, to forgive, and even to
respect." "Not even George Eliot shows such reverence
for average human nature as Mrs. Gaskell; and this is
evident from her earliest work." Although MB had a
great social impact it was not written by one who

chiefly sought effect from art but by a writer "possessed
with and drenched in her subject."

1956

100 Hopewell, Donald. "Two Literary Ladies; Mrs. Gaskell
     and Miss Brontë," Brontë Society Transactions 13
     no. 1 (Part 66), 3-9.

     Compares lives and works of these writers.

101 Thompson, Patricia. The Victorian Heroine: A Changing
     Ideal 1837-1873. London: Oxford University Press,
     pp. 132ff. and passim.

     A study of the rise of feminism in the nineteenth
     century. EG was not an outstanding feminist. For
     example, she was not an ardent supporter of the Married
     Woman's Property Bill, nor did she uphold any "lofty
     ideas about the dignity of female labour." She did,
     however, cast light on the conditions of "unfortunate
     women" like Esther, the prostitute in MB, and Ruth,
     the unmarried mother in R.

     R: The novel, an "artistic achievement on a moral
     theme," inspired violent critical reaction when published
     in 1853. This reaction gives "a revealing picture of
     the ethical background of England at the time." New
     in the book was the attention paid the unmarried mother,
     who was portrayed in the manner of the "virgin heroine."
     EG raised the "question of the comparative importance
     of sins," setting an "inadvertant moral lapse" below
     an "ingrained, fanatical intolerance." The illegitimate
     child was not seen as "a badge of shame" but rather as
     a "purifying influence on the mother." The lover, Mr.
     Bellingham (who later reappears in the story as Mr.
     Donne) is condemned and Faith and Mr. Benson are made
     to shine as examples of Christian charity others should
     emulate. R was a forerunner of Hardy's Tess. In
     Hardy's day, however, "the discussion was now open;
     women showed an undisguised interest in the moral con-
     troversy that was raging, there was no chance of Tess
     being suppressed, like Ruth, as unfit reading for
     mothers. The easy dog-days of masculine tolerance of
     their own shortcomings were almost over, and the exacting
     feminine planet was in the ascendancy at last."

1957

102 Forster, E.M. "Great Writers Rediscovered: The Charm

of Mrs. Gaskell," <u>Sunday Times</u>(London) 7 April,
10-11.

(Not seen.)

03   Halls, Catharine M.E.   "Bibliography of Elizabeth C.
        Gaskell." London Diploma of Librarianship.
        Unpub. Diss. (University of London).

   This bibliography is designed to update to 1956
the two bibliographies published in 1929 by A.S.
Whitfield, 6, and by Clark S. Northup in Sanders, 5.

   The bibliography is arranged in six categories:
Bibliography; Works; Letters; Biography and Criticism;
Supplement to C.S. Northup's and A.S. Whitfield's
bibliographies of Mrs. Gaskell, 1848-1929; Errata in
Northup's bibliography. The Index contains references
to title of works, to editions, to translators, to
authors of books and articles on EG, to universities
listing theses, and to titles of periodicals.

04   Short, Clarice.   "Studies in Gentleness," <u>Western</u>
        <u>Humanities Review</u> 11, 387-93.

   In this comparison of EG's <u>C</u> and Sarah Orne
Jewett's <u>The Country of Pointed Firs</u>(1896) it is noted
that "perhaps both books have lived, in spite of their
lack of plot and sensational action, for three reasons:
the style in which they are written, the use of various
devices to give an impression of life where there is
actually little going on, and the inclusion of various
events which provide us with a kind of wish fulfillment."

05   Shusterman, David.   "William Rathbone Greg and Mrs.
        Gaskell," <u>Philological Quarterly</u> 36, 268-72.

   Proposes William Rathbone Greg, in place of James
Nasmyth, as the more likely model for John Thornton,
the Milton-Northern manufacturer, in <u>NS</u>.

1958

106   Bell, Inglis F. and Donald Baird.   <u>The English Novel</u>
        <u>1578-1956</u>: A <u>Checklist of Twentieth Century</u>
        <u>Criticism</u>. Denver: Alan Swallow, pp. 53-55.

   A listing of books and periodicals cricitising

EG's work.

107 Brightfield, Myron F.   "Introduction" to Mary Barton.
        New York: W.W. Norton and Company Inc., pp. v-xiii.
        The Norton Library, no. 10.   "Select Bibliography,"
        p. xiii.   (See 243.)

        In MB "Mrs. Gaskell has blended the 'social' and
     the 'novel' elements into the organic union of a
     soundly integrated plot.   Through this achievement
     she, in greater measure than her rivals in the field,
     awarded artistic validity to the type" of the social-
     problem novel.

108 Clark, Alexander P.   "The Manuscript Collections of the
        Princeton University Library: An Introductory
        Survey," Princeton University Library Chronicle
        19, 159-90.   EG p. 167.

        "The collection has . . . significant groups of
     letters and manuscripts of Charlotte Brontë, Louise
     de la Ramée (Ouida), Charles Dickens, George Du Maurier,
     Mrs. Gaskell, George Meredith, and W.M. Thackeray."

109 ffrench, Yvonne.   "Elizabeth Cleghorn Gaskell," in
        From Jane Austen to Joseph Conrad: Essays Col-
        lected in Memory of James T. Hillhouse.   Edited
        by Robert C. Rathburn and Martin Steinmann, Jr.
        Minneapolis: University of Minnesota Press, pp.
        133-45.

        Repeats the critical judgments of 74.

110 Hopkins, Annette Brown.   The Father of the Brontës.
        Baltimore, Maryland: The John Hopkins Press.

        "My interest in the Reverend Patrick Brontë arose
     because of his relations with Mrs. Gaskell in the course
     of the writing of her book [LCB] and of the public's
     reception of it.   While I was engaged on my biography,
     [85], I discovered that his correspondence with her re-
     vealed qualities in the man that writers on the Brontës
     had either overlooked or apparently failed to see the
     significance of."

111 Kettle, Arnold.   "The Early Victorian Social-Problem
        Novel," in From Dickens to Hardy, Vol. 6 of The

Pelican Guide to English Literature. Edited by
Boris Ford. Baltimore, Maryland: Penguin Books
Inc., pp. 169-87.

The descriptive label, "social-problem novel,"
could include novels by Godwin as well as by EG. The
difference between the earlier and later novels lies
in changes of tone and subject matter brought about
by the extent of poverty in England in the 1840's.
"While the earlier novelists had seen themselves as
part of a movement of rational reform, their successors
are more often concerned to assert a sense of humane
feeling and solidarity against a vast structure of
rationalized inhumanity."

EG's MB and NS both deal with the Condition-of-
England Question, but they differ principally in the
point of view EG espouses. MB's strength lies in its
accurate portrayal of "working-class life." Her
status as a "district visitor" gave EG a genuine
advantage in portraying the character of working-class
men and women. She sees that Disraeli's "two nations"
definitely exist in England, and succeeds in showing
how this class separation destroys the members of the
working-class. The pattern of separation found in MB
is even reinforced by a minor character like the pros-
titute, Esther, who is "something other than merely a
bad girl; the abyss into which she falls is the same
gulf which separates Dives from Lazarus." While MB
has some weaknesses it remains a powerful novel because
EG portrayed John Barton with great insight and understanding. "Apart from Heathcliff, he is the nearest
approach to a tragic hero which the early Victorian
novel permitted itself."

NS, on the other hand, takes a middle-class stance
in its discussion of the Condition-of-England Question.
The main contrast is not between "rich and poor" but
"between rural and industrial England." NS, while "an
interesting social document . . . lacks the passion"
which "informs" MB. This may be because EG failed "to
bring to bear on agricultural England the same sort of
conscientious insight which she brings to her descriptions of Manchester."

112 Kovalev, Y.V. "The Literature of Chartism: Chartist
        Literature Through Russian Eyes," Victorian Studies
        2, 117-38. Translation by J.C. Dumbreck of the
        Introduction to An Anthology of Chartist Literature,
        com. by Y.V. Kovalev. Moscow: Foreign Languages
        Publishing House, 1956; London: Central Books, 1957.

Rev. by F.C. Mather in <u>Victorian</u> <u>Studies</u> 2, 178-80.

Chartist literature "enriched English literature"
by forcing "writers to see life from a new point of
view." Without them Dickens', Thackeray's and EG's
"inspired visions . . . would have been unthinkable
and the 'graphic and eloquent descriptions' which 'laid
bare to the world more political and social truths
than all the politicians, journalists, and moralists
together have done' would have been impossible.'"

The "legacy" of Chartist literature, which was
"really born" in 1838-39 from the "very character of
the Chartist movement and . . . Chartist ideology,"
cannot be understood without an examination of the
movement in England of "English critical realism." In
the years 1847-8 novels by Dickens(<u>Dombey</u> <u>and</u> <u>Son</u>),
Thackeray(<u>Vanity</u> <u>Fair</u>), Charlotte Brontë(<u>Jane</u> <u>Eyre</u>) and
EG(<u>MB</u>) "were a concentrated blow against anti-realistic
and anti-democratic art. It was in these years that
critical realism became the dominating trend in English
literature." Chartist writers' responses to Dickens
and Thackeray were complex. They did attempt "to work
out their own realistic method," but "they did not
produce any literary manifesto of any kind."

113 Sinclair, May. "Introduction" to <u>The</u> <u>Life</u> <u>of</u> <u>Charlotte</u>
       <u>Brontë</u>. London: J.M. Dent & Sons, Ltd; New York:
       E.P. Dutton & Co., Inc., pp. viii-xiii. Everyman's
       Library, no. 318. (See 293.)

       Standard biographical sketch.

114 Ward, A.C. "Introduction" and "Notes" to <u>Cranford</u>.
       London: Longman's, Green & Co. Heritage of
       Literature Series, ed. by E.W. Parker--Section
       B--no. 33. (See 279.)

       (Not seen.)

115 Williams, Raymond. "The Industrial Novels: <u>Mary</u> <u>Barton</u>
       and <u>North</u> <u>and</u> <u>South</u>, Mrs. Gaskell; <u>Hard</u> <u>Times</u>,
       Dickens; <u>Sybil</u>, Disraeli; <u>Alton</u> <u>Locke</u>, Kingsley;
       <u>Felix</u> <u>Holt</u>, George Eliot," in <u>Culture</u> <u>and</u> <u>Society</u>
       <u>1780-1950</u>. London: Chatto & Windus, pp. 87-109.
       Essay reprinted in <u>The</u> <u>Victorian</u> <u>Novel:</u> <u>Modern</u>
       <u>Essays</u> <u>in</u> <u>Criticism</u>. Edited by Ian Watt. London:
       New York, Oxford: Oxford University Press, 1971,
       pp. 142-64.

Examines MB and NS in order to show that EG evades
an objective analysis of class conflict. In the first
chapters of MB, EG succeeds in recreating "the feel
of everyday life in the working-class homes;" however,
the "structure of feeling" introduced at the start of
the novel changes, owing in part to her publishers'
request to change the title and focus of the book from
"John" to "Mary Barton." But more probably this change
in emphasis indicates that EG could not resolve a
deeper personal conflict. "The real explanation,
surely, is that John Barton, a political murderer . . .
is a dramatization of the fear of violence which was
widespread among upper and middle classes at the time."
EG, at first, meant to examine this fear of the lower
classes, "and the murder of Harry Carson is an imaginative
working-out of this fear, and of reactions to it."
But EG could not come to terms with the situation of
the murder. In consequence she provides a "characteristic humanitarian conclusion" by reconciling Carson
and John Barton, but she removes the remaining characters, the "objects of her real sympathy," far from
the "situation she had set out to examine."

This pattern of evading the objective analysis of
class conflict is shown to occur again in NS. EG
resorts to the riot scene, in which Margaret Hale is
struck down on Thornton's porch, to shift emphasis
away from the scene of confrontation to the particular
concerns of her central characters.

1959

116 Altick, Richard D. "Dion Boucicault Stages Mary Barton,"
     Nineteenth Century Fiction 14, 129-41.

The Long Strike, a "domestic drama" inspired by
MB, was one of three plays written and produced in 1866
by Boucicault for the purpose of winning a wager. To
compare the "dramatic version with the novel offers an
instructive glimpse of the ways of the Victorian stage
adapter." One also gains a new perspective on the
novel after seeing it from the point of view of the
"shrewd but practical dramatist."

Boucicault "seized upon the story alone, improved
it, and made it the substance of an acting play, thus
restoring it to the medium to which, one feels, it was
best suited in the first place. In doing so, he sacri-
ficed nearly all of Mrs. Gaskell's other concerns, such
as social commentary and depth of characterization."
"The Long Strike is much more satisfying as a demon-

stration of the special art of the sensational play
than <u>Mary Barton</u> is as an example of serious fiction."

117   Stang, Richard. <u>The Theory of the Novel in England</u>
           <u>1850-1870</u>. New York: Columbia University Press;
           London: Routledge & Kegan Paul, pp. 70-71, 217
           and <u>passim</u>.

           EG was one of the few "didactic" novelists in the
1850's who avoided complete condemnation by critics.
A novel like <u>R</u> succeeded because it portrayed human
nature and did not deal in abstractions. Yet neither
she nor anyone else was immune to criticism. "Every
important novelist of the period . . . was attacked
. . . for lowering the standard of 'purity' of the
English novel: Dickens and Bulwer for their treatment
of crime and extramarital unions; Thackeray for his
fondness in general for 'unpleasant' subjects, especially
the suggestion of incest in <u>Henry Esmond</u>; Mrs. Gaskell
for dealing with such social questions as the plight
of the unmarried mother in <u>Ruth</u>, prostitution in <u>Mary</u>
<u>Barton</u>, and the condition of the Manchester factory
hands."

                         1960

118   Allott, Miriam. <u>Elizabeth Gaskell</u>. London: Longmans,
           Green & Co. (Writers and their Work, no. 124.)
           "A Select Bibliography," pp. 43-46.

           "Not one of our major novelists," EG's "way of
looking at life is restricted by the limitations of
her intellect and imagination, and her narrative technique is not always free from cliché. . . . She tried
to 'instruct and delight,' in accordance with a critical
precept which is no longer fashionable."

           Short stories: Flawed by "faults of melodrama"
and by "sentimentality" these stories are "still highly
readable." At least they succeeded in their "chief
purpose--to keep the pot boiling and provide a Victorian
lady with pin money."

           <u>MB</u>: EG was probably unaware how sharp an "indict-
ment of <u>laissez faire</u> economics" she made through her
hero, John Barton. Her "great technical triumph,"
portraying the series of events from Carson's murder
to Jem Wilson's trial at Liverpool, is "an achievement
that owes nothing to her 'social purpose.'" EG's
success in <u>MB</u> rests in the "total effect of honesty

                         44

within the limits of a rather conventional understanding."

NS: This novel is perhaps more interesting than MB on account of the principals, who achieve "a strong personal relationship in spite of wide differences." The situation in NS looks not backward but forward "to the emotional entanglements of a later age" characteristic of a novelist like D.H. Lawrence.

R: Modern readers might forget EG's pioneering effort in R, "especially in exposing the double moral standard for men and women." Also they may feel that her "infatuation with emotional cliché makes her treatment of Ruth almost indistinguishable in its moral tone from, say, Dickens's treatment of Little Emily in David Copperfield." She does make "convincing" Ruth's "essential innocence" by "suggesting a harmony between the experience of passion and the beauty of the physical world."

SL: Features of the novel are the accurate representation of dialect and the complexity of characterization. The story should have closed when Sylvia rejects Kinraid, for "the plot runs wild" in the last eleven chapters.

C: A reader is struck anew by C's "tact of presentation" and "the happy discretion of its style." C is "a small masterpiece achieved through emotional understatement, the manner exactly suited to the matter." C works because it appeals to a deep wish in the human makeup. In her Preface to C, Lady Ritchie, Thackeray's daughter, accounted for its enduring popularity by saying "'We all have a Cranford somewhere in our lives'. She meant that in some moods we should all like to have one."

CP: This "short idyll with Wordsworthian overtones, is more subtle in feeling" than C. It is one of EG's "finest pieces of prose."

WD: EG's "masterpiece." This is the "only novel (Cranford is a series of sketches) which a contemporary reader will feel at home with." While part of the novel might have autobiographical overtones (Molly's relationship with Mrs. Gibson, her stepmother) EG's "imaginative insight" is more striking than any employment of autobiographical elements.

LCB: A "remarkable" portrait. Her novelist's skills permitted her to tell more about Charlotte and Emily Brontë "than she intended."

119   Altick, Richard D. and William R. Matthews, com.
      Guide to Doctoral Dissertations in Victorian
      Literature. Urbana: University of Illinois Press,
      pp. 53-54.

      Lists dissertations having to do with EG.

120   Gaskell Committee, Urban District Council, Knutsford,
      England. Knutsford and Mrs. Gaskell. Derby and
      Cheltenham: New Centurion Publishing Co., 1960.
      Privately printed pamphlet.

      (Not seen.)

121   Grossman, L. "Mrs. Gaskell's influence on Dostoevsky,"
      Voprosi Literaturi 4 (1959); trans. in Anglo-Soviet
      Journal 21 (1960).

      (Not seen.)

122   Stevenson, Lionel. The English Novel: A Panorama.
      Boston: Houghton Mifflin Company (The Riverside
      Press, Cambridge), pp. 279ff.

      Although her social novels were influential, EG
      wrote best about the domestic scene. Her fiction does
      not exhibit the same intellectual maturity that Meredith
      and Eliot achieved in their works. By 1859 fiction had
      arrived at intellectual maturity. The religious code
      of morality weakened and human nature was opened to
      scientific analysis. The novel by the 1860's had
      reached a plateau.

      MB: "The handling of the story is amateurish,
      falling back on melodramatic action to sustain interest,
      and sometimes condensing a crucial scene into flat
      exposition." "As a social treatise it is invalidated
      by the author's naïve optimism." Yet, EG had "the
      essential power of creating characters who enlist the
      reader's emotional participation." Unlike Mrs. Trollope
      in Michael Armstrong or Harriet Martineau, EG was the
      first to treat social concerns "in the simple light
      of common humanity."

      C: The story is "rudimentary in plot and so
      closely based on reminiscence that it can be admitted
      only marginally to the genre of the novel." "It is
      the most placid book in English fiction." It survives
      because in it EG never "degenerates into sentimentality"

46

and because "its events, trivial though they are,
capture something of the pathos inherent in ordinary
people." C's "special significance" is that it is "a
symptom of the triumph of domestic tranquillity as a
fictional mode."

R: A "startingly unconventional" book, R and the
earlier MB nonetheless are so inferior to C "that they
seem like the work of a different author." In both
EG was writing outside her range. R is a "sort of
fairy tale made up by a sensitive child who has heard
about a world in which painful things happen." However, the book did help to stir Josephine Butler "to
take the lead in reforming English laws regarding
prostitution and in seeking to control the 'white
slave traffic.'"

NS: One observes an advance in EG's powers of
execution in this book. "The distress of the poor is
presented through experiences of the characters rather
than by the author's disquisitions." Her solution,
however, remains the same as that in MB and "her
attempt to be tolerant to all parties deprives the
story of any strong appeal to the reader's moral judgment."

SL and WD: Both books illustrate the "growth of
realism in the domestic novel." EG had "relinquished
social propaganda and settled down to the more tran-
quil mood of Cranford." SL is "not much more of a
historical novel than Adam Bede." WD "her longest
book" is "almost devoid of action" but is certainly
her "masterpiece."

123   Townsend, John R. "Mrs Gaskell--Radical," The Manchester
          Guardian 28 Sept., 9.

The article notes the celebrations at Knutsford
marking the one hundred fiftieth anniversary of EG's
birth (29 Sept.).

The author also appraises the current state of
Gaskell criticism. The popularity of C has hurt EG's
image and it may have conditioned Cecil's, 28, critical
opinion, which has proven to be wildly wrong. She
deserves reconsideration, particularly in regards to
her Northern novels and the experience from which they
were produced. NS "her most remarkable novel" provides
the "key" to EG's "character." In this book one finds
a partial self-portrait in the genteelly bred Southern
girl moving to a grim Northern city, where she gradually

learns to appreciate and admire Northern virtues of
industry and command "without ever being fully assi-
milated." With this key one can see why she wrote so
fine a biography of CB. In LCB she combined "a powerful gift for topographical writing" with an understanding
of "Charlotte and Emily who belong body and soul to
the North."

1961

124 Allott, Miriam. "Mrs. Gaskell's 'The Old Nurse's
        Story': A Link between 'Wuthering Heights' and
        'The Turn of the Screw'," N&Q NS 8 [206], 101-2.

   EG takes images and atmosphere from Wuthering
Heights. Henry James' use of the governess is shown
to be derived in part from EG's.

125 Chadwick, Esther Alice. "Introduction" to North and
        South. London: J.M. Dent & Sons Ltd; New York:
        E.P. Dutton & Co., Inc. Everyman's Library, no.
        680. Reissue of edition first published in 1914.
        (See 287.)

   (Not seen.)

126 Laski, Marghanita. "Words from Mrs. Gaskell," N&Q NS
        8 [206], 339-41. See also N&Q NS 8 [206], 468-69,
        and N&Q NS 9 [207] (Jan. 1962), 27-28.

   EG's works provide a "surprising number of ante-
datings and unlisted words" for a reader for the Oxford
English Dictionary.

127 Maison, Margaret M. The Victorian Vision: Studies
        in the Religious Novel. New York: Sheed & Ward,
        pp. 202-3.

   When she visited England, Harriet Beecher Stowe
met EG, who much admired her work. The success of
Uncle Tom's Cabin "doubtless inspired Mrs. Gaskell
to turn from the exquisite enchantments of Cranford
to produce another explosive novel, and Ruth (1853)"
was the shocking result. The clash in R between two
faiths, "enlightened compassionate Christianity (showing
the 'highest charity' of which Miss Martineau wrote),
and narrow rigid Pharisaical Nonconformity, makes this
a most stimulating religious novel." EG stresses the

"creative" not the "punitive" power of Christianity
throughout her work.

28   Pollard, Arthur.   "The Novels of Mrs. Gaskell," Bulletin
          of the John Rylands Library Manchester 43, 403-25.
          "Appendix: Gaskell Manuscript Material in
          Manchester," pp. 424-25.

          In this discussion of C, MB, NS, SL and WD, it is
     observed that in the last two novels, SL and WD, "there
     is a new technical control, a deeper investigation of
     individual behaviour, a fresh awareness of the intensity
     of human passions." Of her it "may certainly be said
     that she died in the fulness of her powers."

29   Pollard, Arthur.   "'Sooty Manchester' and the Social-
          reform Novel 1845-1855: An examination of Sybil,
          Mary Barton, North and South, and Hard Times,"
          British Journal of Industrial Medecine, 18, 85-92.
          A paper given to the Thackrah Club in Manchester
          18 Nov. 1960.

          "Possessed of a knowledge, or more correctly of
     a sort of knowledge, to which neither Dickens nor
     Disraeli could lay claim, [EG] delineated accurately
     the Manchester she knew so well." Because Manchester
     was growing so rapidly, and the lack of parks was
     recognized and lamented, EG's opening of MB in Green
     Heys Fields is all the more effective. EG and Dickens,
     unlike Disraeli, wrote little about the aristocracy;
     the "chief interest of all three novelists lies,
     however, in the middle and lower classes, the manu-
     facturers and workmen, and the constant struggle be-
     tween them." At times the novelist will fit his
     characters to a plan--Dickens was "prone" to this--
     but EG treated only her secondary characters, like
     Esther in MB, this way.

          The novelists failed to effect any real alteration
     or "clear away the incongruities of inescapable reality;"
     yet their failure does not detract from the "intense
     sympathy with suffering mankind and a strong desire
     for the amelioration of the human condition," which
     inspired them.

                           1962

30   Billingsley, Bruce Alder.   "'Take Her Up Tenderly':
          A Study Of The Fallen Woman In The Nineteenth-

Century English Novel." <u>DA</u> 23,1681-82 (University of Texas).

Treats the "fallen woman" theme, "a generic term, including all women guilty of sexual impropriety," as an increasingly important theme in the Victorian novel. It is shown that this theme appeared in one novel by every major English novelist of the century, that it has a "traceable" evolution, and that the novels had an immediate influence upon the reading public.

In <u>R</u>, a novel of "mixed excellence," EG treats her subject with the "melodrama" still conventionally associated with the treatment of the theme. She makes her appeal for Ruth on a religious basis, the safest available, but she "miscalculated" the public temper. Nonetheless, the book broke ground, and a more "disturbing" book on the subject did not appear, perhaps, until Hardy's <u>Tess</u>.

131 Shain, Charles E. "The English Novelists and the American Civil War," <u>American Quarterly</u> 14, 399-421.

A quotation from a letter from EG to Charles Eliot Norton, asking him to explain the cause of the Civil War to "average" English people like the Gaskells, is used to introduce this essay, which canvasses British literary reactions to the war.

                              1963

132 Allott, Miriam. "Great Writers-11: Mrs. Gaskell," <u>Time and Tide</u> 14-20 Mar., 21-22.

Repeats in abridged form 118. EG's works reflect a "sanguine equable temperament." Her best works are <u>C</u>, <u>CP</u>, WD and <u>LCB</u>, but the "social" novels <u>MB</u>, <u>R</u>, <u>NS</u>, too, reflect "the good intentions and modest insight of the decent 'aroused' citizen, and she does this without the stridency which usually accompanies our 'kitchen sink' writing today."

133 Dodsworth, Martin. "Women Without Men at Cranford," <u>Essays in Criticism</u> 13, 132-45.

Critics tend to overlook the "psychological accuracy" of <u>C</u>. "The fundamentally serious concerns of her book have been neglected for a belle-lettriste study of

incidental detail." Critics also look in the wrong
places. "The force of the novel lies in plot . . .
not in character."

"Instead of treating <u>Cranford</u> as the literal
representation of a series of actions that might really
have taken place, [the critic] must rid his mind altogether of the knowledge that some of them did in fact
take place, and treat the novel as symbolic of a conflict within the mind of the author. <u>Cranford</u> is a
kind of trimmed and tidied dream, in which Mrs. Gaskell's
unconscious hostility to the male struggles with her
awareness of the pointlessness of such hostility in
the predominately masculine society of her day."

EG explores the essential sterility of the pose
of "gentility" in Cranford, showing how it is responsible for sexual frustration in Miss Matty, who gives
up her lover for her sister's sake, and in Peter Jenkyns,
who in a "bizarre transvestite episode . . . dresses
up as his sister Deborah, and pretends to be nursing
a baby (a taunt at her unmarried state)." Female gentility succeeds in evicting male vitality from Cranford,
for a time. The hysteria of the ladies, caused by
imagined robbers, has a frankly "sexual aspect," however,
and is an admission of "the women's feeling of helpless-
ness" in the face of the unknown. This permits the
reintroduction into Cranford of "the principle of male
vitality" which brings with it "promise of new life."

"Her style . . . is one that is extremely lucid
and direct; there is no fumbling." "The unambiguous
prose insists that we should believe" and her "direct
appeal to emotion is all the more effective for Mrs.
Gaskell's not 'writing it up'." Style and form are inter-
woven for "the form of the novel is carefully chosen too.
The fact that it is a pastoral, in which Cranford gains
emotional significance by contrast with the industrial
town of Drumble, is admirably in harmony with its being
a verbalized equivalent of dream. The master-stroke
is putting the story into a first-person narrative.
Mary Smith, of whose speaking voice we are made con-
stantly aware, casts a totally subjective aura over
the action." By identifying, through the narrator, with
the "author of the story," we are "led to feel, at an
unconscious level, the unity of her book."

.34 Sharps, John G. "Charlotte Brontë and the Mysterious
          'Miss H.': A Detail in Mrs. Gaskell's <u>Life</u>,"
          <u>English</u> 14, 236.

The reference to "Miss H.," which occurs in a
letter written by Charlotte Brontë to Ellen Nussey in
EG's LCB [V. 1(1st ed.), ch. 9, p. 218], was actually
a substitution made by EG herself for the original words
"the Miss Woolers." EG had great respect for one Mrs.
John Wade (née Sarah Hartley), who was "instrumental
in obtaining for Charlotte Brontë the post of governess
with Mr. and Mrs. White at Rawdon." EG paid her a
compliment by using the "initial from Mrs. Wade's maiden
name" in her biography.

1964

135 Barry, James D. "Elizabeth Cleghorn Gaskell [and]
         Charles Kingsley," Victorian Fiction: A Guide to
         Research. Edited by Lionel Stevenson. Cambridge,
         Massachusetts: Harvard University Press, pp.
         245-76. EG pp. 245-63.

         Provides a listing of major bibliographies, editions,
letters, biographies and other studies of EG. Since
"the attention given her in recent times is short of
what her contemporary fame would lead us to expect"
it is clear that there is a "need for an overall critical
study of Mrs. Gaskell's fiction and a reassessment of
her position both within Victorian fiction and within
English fiction as a whole."

136 Carnall, Geoffrey. "Dickens, Mrs. Gaskell, and the
         Preston Strike," Victorian Studies 7, 31-48.

         Compares Dickens' Hard Times to EG's NS. "Mrs.
Gaskell's treatment of industrial relations illustrates
her shrewd insight into the mixture of exasperation
and sympathy which enters into most people's feelings
for each other. Dickens is less interested in the way
people interact. His characters tend to be insulated
individuals, artistes in a music hall rather than actors
in a comedy."

         EG and Dickens differ in their attitudes toward
"lying." "Margaret is untruthful for a good reason,
but the violence which she does to her own nature in
telling the lie reflects something of Mrs. Gaskell's
own constraint in the act of invention."

137 Holloway, S.W.F. "Medical Education in England, 1830-
         1858: A Sociological Analysis," History 49,
         299-324.

In 1834 it is estimated that 3,500 or 41% of the
surgeons practicing in England were "members of the
College of Surgeons and held in addition the license
of the Society of Apothecaries." The additional license
protected surgeons against certain penalties of law.
But not all surgeons made the effort to obtain a license
from the Apothecaries' Hall. "Mr. Gibson, in Elizabeth
Gaskell's novel Wives and Daughters, had a good general
practice in the country yet only held a surgeon's
diploma."

138 Hulin, Jean-Paul. "Les débuts littéraires de Mrs.
        Gaskell: Réflexions sur un poème oublié," Études
        Anglaises 17, 128-39.

     Suggests that EG's ideas for MB sprang predominantly
from research she performed for her husband in 1838,
when he was composing a series of lectures on the
subject "The Poets and the Poetry of Humble Life."
Further, a hitherto unattributed poem, "Rich and Poor,"
published in The North of England Magazine (May 1842),
is attributed to EG because its subject matter coincides
with her political and social attitudes and reflects
ideas that appear in MB. The character of the poem
(printed in full in the essay) suggests that MB "fut
le produit d'une lente maturation, d'un réflexion
prolongée sur des conflits sociaux particulièrement
observables à Manchester."

139 Pollard, Arthur. "Introduction" to Sylvia's Lovers.
        London: J.M. Dent & Sons Ltd, pp. v-ix. Everyman's
        Library, no. 524. "Select Bibliography," p. ix.
        (See 299.)

     "In this novel of love and jealousy, hatred,
revenge and ultimate forgiveness Mrs Gaskell sought
to deal more massively with the passions than in any
other of her works. It is this which makes comparison
with Wuthering Heights not wholly inappropriate. That
novel however exists only in its own world. It is to
the credit of Sylvia's Lovers that we are able to
believe that it exists in ours."

                          1965

140 Brill, Barbara. "Getting To Know Elizabeth Gaskell,"
        Library Review 20, 227-33.

     "The discovery of Elizabeth Gaskell through the

                          53

reading of her books and the acquaintance I have made
through her pages of many varied characters have enriched
my life as much as the making of new personal friends.
. . . I feel a pang of sorrow at the thought that but
for her untimely death Mrs Gaskell would have created
still more characters for me to meet in the pages of
those novels that will never be written."

141   Carwell, Virginia Alice.   "Serialization And The Fiction
        of Mrs. Gaskell." DA 26, 3328 (Northwestern
        University).

        Takes a "chronological approach" in a study of
the influences of serialization on EG's literary performance. Serialization did little harm to shorter
works, save DNW, where a break in the center spoils
the suspense. The weekly publication schedule of HW
and the fact that NS was incomplete when installments
first appeared contributed to the unhappy history and
"muddled" ending of that book. The monthly installment
pattern of the Cornhill Magazine contributed to EG's
satisfactory performance in WD.

        "All the evidence indicates that publication form
in the nineteenth century was indeed a significant
matter for almost any author. What was true in general
was especially true for Mrs. Gaskell. If her short
pieces were more or less independent of serial influences,
the longer works were not: effects might be temporary
or permanent, negative or positive, but for longer works
by Mrs. Gaskell [NS and WD], serialization did make
a difference."

142   Edwards, Olive.   "The Story of A Lie," Times (London)
        2 Sept., 5.

        An appreciation of SL. "I know of no novel of an
earlier generation that so perfectly foreshadows
[Hardy's] own masterpieces." Her northern characters
are as true "as his Wessex ones," and "while Mrs.
Gaskell's faith was given to something more numinous
than a President of the Immortals, she allowed Fate to
have a cruel implacability even if she disguised it
as retribution." To those who criticize the ending
of SL, it must be remembered that she was an experi-
menter in the novel tradition and that the ending is
effective still today. The whole story derives its
strength from the integrity of the characters portrayed.

43   Edwards, Tudor. "Portrait of Knutsford: The Cranford
         of Mrs. Gaskell," Country Life 138, 1274-77.

        Celebrates EG's centenary with descriptions and
some photographs of Knutsford buildings associated with
EG's life and described in her fiction.

44   Gaskell, E.C. "A Letter From Mrs. Gaskell," Brontë
         Society Transactions 14 no. 5 (Part 75), 50.

        The Society prints the text of a letter from EG
to the Rev. R.S. Oldham, of Glasgow, written 1 June
1857, which it purchased in March of this year. Of
interest is the picture it gives of EG's "reactions
after the publication" of LCB.

45   Gross, John. "Early-Victorian writer with charm,"
         Listener 73, 361-63. Reprinted as "Mrs. Gaskell,"
         in The Novelist as Innovator. Ed., and intro.
         by Walter Allen. London: British Broadcasting
         Corporation, 1965, pp. 46-93; also, in The Vic-
         torian Novel: Modern Essays in Criticism. Edited
         by Ian Watt. London, New York, Oxford: Oxford
         University Press, 1971, pp. 217-28.

        "To appreciate Mrs. Gaskell fully one must try to
see her work as a whole, to understand how Cranford,
with its muslin and bonnets and filigree sugar-tongs,
can be sandwiched in between Mary Barton and North and
South--novels full of gloom and violence."

        MB: "Mrs. Gaskell's great virtue was that she
was interested in the People as people, that she had
a gossipy curiosity about their daily lives. And she
kept a cool head--the first thing which strikes one
about Mary Barton is its composure." EG's "express
purpose was to win respect for her characters," and to
this end she employed a "documentary element" and
provided footnotes explaining any "Lancashire dialect
word or construction."

        NS: As a "social document" . . . NS is more
"cautious, more evasive" than MB. "But as a novel it
is more revolutionary, since the author has a deeper
personal stake in it and deliberately uses a more
sophisticated narrative technique. She is no longer
the detached observer, the well-disposed district
visitor; through the consciousness of Margaret she
allows the world which she describes to impinge directly
upon her." "The book is resolutely modern, particularly

in its insistence that 'you can't go home again.'" The
novel looks forward in another way. Its most original
feature is "the idea of sexual excitement being entwined
with social antagonism." There is even a suggestion
of "race-antagonism in [John Thornton's] relationship
with Margaret."

C: "Cranford is indestructible: it has the
confidence, the grace, the rightness which can only
come when an author is writing out of an unimpeded
imagination, and writing about the things that matter
most to him." In its own indirect way it is as much
a statement on the Condition of England question as MB
or NS. When a bank failure deprives Miss Matty of
an income the Cranford ladies may be "parochial and
prim" but they know what they must do, and they all
"rally round." Despite the small hypocrisies in
upholding "elegant economy" in Cranford, it has a
"sounder heart than political economy." Mary Smith
learns the true worth of Cranford values. But she herself is a modern girl and belongs to Drumble, as
Margaret Hale at the close of NS belongs to Milton.

Despite her Thackeray-like sensitivity to "the
passage of time" EG knew how to handle early Victorian
nostalgia "tactfully." Few writers could have written
a chapter so effective as that in which Miss Matty and
Mary sort family letters before destroying them.

146   Handley, Graham. "The Chronology of Sylvia's Lovers,"
      N&Q NS 12 [210], 302-3.

      Notes "errors in point of time" in SL.

147   Pollard, Arthur. Mrs Gaskell Novelist and Biographer.
      Cambridge, Mass.: Harvard University Press.

      Rev. by John Daniel in Spectator 22 Oct., 518;
      by Naomi Lewis in New York Times Book Review 20 Nov.,
      36; by Margaret Drabble in Manch. Guard. Weekly 1
      Dec., 11; by John Gross in New York Review of Books
      29 Dec., 21-22; by V.S. Pritchett in New Statesman
      NS 71 (1966), 16; in TLS 13 Jan. (1966), 26; by Rosamund
      Lehmann in Listener 125 (1966), 107; by K.J. Fielding
      in N&Q NS 13 [211] (1966), 355-56; (with other works)
      by Alexander Welsh in Yale Review 56 (1966), 152-56;
      by Graham Handley in Durham University Journal NS
      27 [58] (1966), 164-67; by Gilbert Thomas in English
      16 (1966), 66-67; by H. Coombes in Essays in Criticism
      16 (1966), 473-89; by Arthur Minerof in Library Journal

91 (1966), 3952; by F. Basch in Études Anglaises 20
(1967), 93-95; by Lionel Stevenson in English Language
Notes 4 (1967), 225-27; by Patricia Thompson in Review
of English Studies NS 18, 218-19; by William F. Axton
in Modern Language Quarterly 28 (1967), 240-47; by John
Lucas in Victorian Studies 11 (1968), 528-33.

By concentrating on "matters of plot, character,
setting, information and moral purposes as separate
entitites within each of Mrs Gaskell's works," Pollard
hopes to "restore" to EG "that degree of favour which
she enjoyed in her lifetime and for some years afterwards." The book begins with a biographical chapter
in which EG is shown to be a many-sided and vibrant
personality whose "qualities as a person are reflected
abundantly in her books." He then proceeds to consider
the works in chronological order.

MB: "Her chief concern was not with economics,
but with human kindness." While the "narrative crudi-
ties of the book" indicate EG's inability to unite her
realistic material with a didactic social message, she
shows her powers as a convincing portraitist of character.

C: On examination the book reveals even deeper
complexities which EG achieves by employing, through
Mary Smith, a "detached" narrative voice. "The detachment of Mary Smith allows for the play of Mrs Gaskell's
tender irony upon the foibles of her characters, whilst
the inclusion of her observer as an actor ensures that
the irony is also partially gentle self-derision."

R: The most deliberately "moral" of her novels.
It is filled with "contrivances" of plotting to point
the moral. In some ways EG shows artistic advances
in R, such as her narrowing her interest to fewer
characters and her concentrating most of her attention
on Ruth herself. But even her treatment of Ruth lacks
the "imaginative energy" exhibited in her drawing of
John Barton.

NS: "The management of plot and character, the
exposition of theme, the variation in direction of
interest, all demonstrate a grasp of the novelist's
technique hitherto undemonstrated." EG has succeeded
in working her "thesis" artistically into NS and what
is more she "has achieved a coalescence between personal
and public stories in the relationship of the two
major characters." NS marks a turning point in her
career as a writer ("Cranford always excepted")
because she decided that the novel must be primarily

about people affecting each other, not about individuals
"affected by social and economic forces."

LCB: A modern reader probably will not be satis-
fied with all aspects of LCB but noone can deny its
worthiness to be "ranked with the great biographies
of English literature."

Shorter stories: EG's earlier short stories suffer
because she could not concentrate her energies and
be brief, as the form demanded. Her later stories,
particularly HLA, LW, and SWH show her deftness as an
artist. The longer "nouvelles," MC, MHC, MLL and CP,
also show artistic change. The first two are early
stories, imperfect but rich in characterization, while
the last two reveal almost perfectly created artistic
worlds. In MLL "she is re-creating the very being of
the society she describes." CP is the "last and best
of her shorter works." In this story we discover "that
perfect spontaneity which marks the consummate artist."

SL: EG's triumph in SL is her power to embody
in Sylvia Robson a profound "concentration of human
experience." In this novel EG approached most closely
the presentation of a story in "epic proportions," and
the "success" of the novel stems from "her understanding
of the essential tragic vision."

WD: The unfinished WD is a story involving very
little action but it signals EG's move into new areas
of characterization. Mrs. Gibson and Cynthia Kirkpatrick show EG operating in a "new subtler and completely unexpected dimension." She writes with "a
moral view of life" but her "more refined, more delicate treatment" of these characters "reminds us of
Jane Austen and of Henry James."

148   Pollard, Arthur. "Mrs. Gaskell's Life of Charlotte
        Brontë," Bulletin of the John Rylands Library
        Manchester 47, 453-88. Includes Albert H. Preston,
        "Appendix: Mrs. Gaskell's Letters to John Greenwood
        regarding the Brontës," pp. 477-88.

      Re-examines EG's difficulties and successes in
      writing LCB.

149   Pollard, Arthur. "Mrs. Gaskell's Short Stories."
        Cambridge Review 8 May.

      (Not seen.)

150   Schneewind, Jerome B. "Moral Problems and Moral
          Philosophy in the Victorian Period," Victorian
          Studies 9, 29-46.

        The understanding of some literary works of the
nineteenth-century may be aided by an understanding
of the philosophical debate between Utilitarians and
Intuitionists in the century. The debate appears in
EG's NS, submerged in the characters of Margaret Hale
and John Thornton. Margaret Hale, possessing an
"Intuitionist conscience," must meet "a world full of
problems" for it. In the face of apologists, her conscience tells her that to lie about her brother was
wrong. But her greatest obstacle is John Thornton, whose
"life and views incarnate the Utilitarianism of the
industrial North." The Intuitionist side conquers
the Utilitarian in the novel, through the agency of
human feeling. Thornton's feelings for Margaret Hale
bring about a change in his "morality."

151   Scotton, John. "Rev. John Jenkyns in Cranford," N&Q
          NS 12 [210], 194.

        Who is the prototype for the character of the Rev.
John Jenkyns in C?

152   Sharps, John G. "Articles by Mrs. Gaskell in 'The
          Pall Mall Gazette' (1865)," N&Q NS 12 [210], 301-2.

        Documents newly discovered articles by EG.

153   Wright, Edgar. "Mrs. Gaskell, A Study Of Her Attitudes
          And Beliefs In Relation To Her Development As A
          Novelist." Unpub. Doc. Diss. (Northwestern
          University).

        (Not seen.)

154   Wright, Edgar. "Mrs. Gaskell and the World of 'Cran-
          ford'," Review of English Literature 6 no. 1,
          68-79.

        "Cranford, I repeat, is not Knutsford but there
is a good deal of Knutsford in Cranford, and Knutsford
was a neighbouring locality where friends lived and
her daughters went to school. It provides a solid
element of normality for imagination and memory to
bite on." In later work, particularly WD, the segment

59

of society pictured in C̲ "has retreated into the background."   But EG, having finally selected the young
and adaptable as the more permanent force in English
life, does not belittle the values, virtues and good-
ness of members of the earlier generation that peopled
Cranford.

155   Wright, Edgar.   Mrs. Gaskell: The Basis for Reassessment.
London, New York: Oxford University Press.
"Appendix: The Original Rough Sketch For
Mary Barton," pp. 265-68. "Bibliography," pp.
269-73. "A Chronological List of Writings of
Mrs. Gaskell," pp. 275-77.

Rev. by John Daniel in Spectator 22 Oct., 518;
by V.S. Pritchett in New Statesman NS 71 (1966), 16;
in TLS 13 Jan. (1966), 26; by Rosamund Lehmann in
Listener 125 (1966), 107; by Graham Handley in Durham
University Journal NS 27 [58] (1966), 164-67; in
Economist 218, 1425; by Gilbert Thomas in English 16,
22-23; by Arnold Kettle in Critical Quarterly 8 (1966),
185-87; by H. Coombes in Essays in Criticism 16 (1966),
473-89; by U. Laredo in English Studies in Africa 9
(1966), 217-19; by F. Basch in Études Anglaises 20
(1967), 93-95; by Rudolph Vallgrandter in Anglia 85
(1967), 229-31; by Jerome Thale in Modern Philology
65 (1967), 170-71; by James D. Barry in Nineteenth
Century Fiction 21 (1967), 395-400; by Patricia Thompson
in Review of English Studies NS 18 (1967), 218-19;
by William F. Axton in Modern Language Quarterly 28
(1967), 240-47; by John Lucas in Victorian Studies 11
(1968), 528-33.

EG's critical reputation to date reveals both
"confusion of approach" and "varying estimates not only
of her work as a whole but of her individual novels."
The "way out" of such confusion and towards "a firmly
based assessment of her achievement, can only be through
a closer examination of what she actually wrote and
of her methods as a novelist." Wright attempts to show
that the growth of the novelist is marked both by a
steadily decreasing didacticism and by an increasing
artistry which culminates in the "final synthesis" of
CP and WD.

EG was a "social novelist" who wrote in the
interest of bringing religion into the lives of those
who did not have it. She focused her attention on
the family, which she saw as the basic social unit.
One acquired stability of character in the family.
"Stability of character is, then, linked with emotional

stability and social stability in the family unit, it
is a conflation that suits Mrs. Gaskell's interests
and whose use she develops steadily." EG became adept
at showing how family weaknesses and strengths determined the attitudes to adversity faced by characters
like Mary Barton, Sylvia Robson and Phillis Holman.

MB, C, NS: In her own life EG became acutely
sensitive to the process of change occuring in England.
At first she tried simply to compare the Manchester
world to the Cranford world in MB and C. In NS she
attempted a "reconciliation" of the social traditions
of the past with the new traditions emerging from the
industrial revolution. Although she makes her character Margaret Hale admit that the South promotes a
"pointless existence in its cities" and a "brutalized
spiritless type of worker" where the North develops
active, vital and practical virtues, her own sympathies
were not with the utilitarian, industrial North. She
projects onto Margaret attributes she feels she herself
should have and attempts "to defeat her prejudices"
against the Manchester world by dealing with them in
fiction, "making the novel a fantasy substitute for a
failure of reality."

LCB: The biography provides an interesting gloss
on her changing techniques and developing artistry.
The materials for the biography suited her because she
was interested in growth and change in complex characters, and analysis of relationships in families.
The major effect of writing the biography was its urging
EG to take a more realistic attitude towards human
life, for CB's life could not be fit to the moral
patterning that determined the plot of many of EG's
earlier stories. EG had to admit she could not "judge"
CB, nor afterwards does she judge her characters in her
best works.

MLL: In MLL EG again took up in the Cranford
manner the theme of traditional ways brought to adjust
to social change. If the story is marred by the inclusion of the story within a story, in other ways
it is an advance beyond C because her social range
and the seriousness of social analysis has greatly
increased. She has found her true theme in MLL, the
focus of attention on "individual adjustment" to the
traditional as well as to the new patterns of society.

LW, SL: LW and SL show EG's deepening concern
with questions of good and evil, and with "morbid
psychology." Both are surprisingly void of humor.
The New England social structure, unstable, inconsiderate

of beauty, destructive of a sensitive girl whose values
have been acquired in a Cranford-like English village,
provided EG a perfect situation to analyze, in historical
perspective, the effects of an unstable and uncohesive
social structure, like that of Manchester, upon individual values. SL further examines the theme of the
"uprooted individual." Her peculiar reversion to
impose a moral, overly religious pattern upon her story
in the third volume can be explained as a sign of reaction to Darwin's theories and Tennyson's questioning
of faith in In Memoriam.

CP, WD: In these books EG returns to the Cranford
world but with a more complex and profound understanding
of that world's values. In her "pastoral elegy,"
CP, EG achieves a natural and effortless manner of
dealing with "fundamental issues" of individual emotions
of love and despair set against a world that is in
many ways stable but whose values are shifting. In
WD EG interweaves, by means of an acquired artistry,
the themes of her previous works into a "final synthesis."

1966

156   Chapple, J.A.V., "Gaskell Letters," TLS 25 Aug., 770.

Announces that "a number of almost completely
unknown letters written to Mrs. Gaskell . . . before
her marriage have recently been found and added to
the Collection of Mr. J.G. Sharps" of Manchester.

157   Chapple, J.A.V. and Arthur Pollard, eds. The Letters
of Mrs Gaskell. Cambridge, Massachusetts: Harvard
University Press; Manchester, England: Manchester
University Press, 1966.

Rev. by Margaret Drabble in Manchester Guardian
Weekly 1 Dec., 11; by Martin Seymour-Smith in Spectator
9 Dec., 760-61; in Economist 221, 1331; (with other
works) by V.S. Pritchett in New Statesman NS 72, 967-68;
by Julian Symons in Listener 77 (1967), 300; by A.B.
Hopkins in Brontë Society Transactions 15 (1967), 151-57;
in TLS 16 Mar. (1967), 209-10 (see 165); by William
F. Axton in Modern Language Quarterly 28 (1967), 240-47;
by John Lucas in Victorian Studies 11 (1968), 528-33;
by K.J. Fielding in Nineteenth Century Fiction 23 (1968),
243-45; by F. Basch in Etudes Anglaises 21 (1968), 257-71;
by Graham Handley in N&Q NS 15 [213] (1968), 438-39;
by Rachael Bush in Journal of Australasian Univ. Lang.
and Lit. Association 29 (1968), 97-98.

The letters cover EG's life "from just before her
marriage" to the week of her death. The volume includes
divisions for dated and undated letters. "Appendix
A: Additional Letters," pp. 814-942, "contains letters
that became available after the edition had reached
the page-proof stage." "Appendix B," pp. 943-45, cites
the "Sources," either the "owner or location" of each
letter. "Appendix C," pp. 946-48, lists "Watermarks."
"Appendix D," pp. 949-50, lists "Embossed Designs."
"Appendix E: Table of Descriptions," pp. 951-66,
provides "recorded information about individual letters
in eight columns . . . which should be read in conjunction with Appendices B, C, and D." "Appendix F:
Miscellaneous," pp. 967-71. The Index is divided into
three parts: 1. "Select Family Index," pp. 972-77;
2. "Literary Index," pp. 977-81; 3. "General Biographical Index," pp. 981-1010.

158 Dick, Kay. "Introduction" to Mary Barton, A Tale of
        Manchester Life. London: Panther Books Ltd.
        (See 244.)

     (Not seen.)

159 Johnson, C.A. "Russian Gaskelliana," Review of English
        Literature 7 no. 3, 39-51.

     Though probably unaware of it herself, EG's R and,
in a more dramatic way, MB had widespread influence
on Russian literature.

     A translation by Mme Beketova of MB appeared in
Fyodor and Mikhail Dostoevsky's magazine Time (Vremya)
in 1861. Before the magazine was closed down they had
begun to publish R. Only one installment of R was
published in Time (no. 4, 1863).

     MB appeared in Time for a variety of reasons.
Fyodor Dostoevsky planned to use his magazine to support a program of reconciliation between classes. MB
was useful because it accorded with his program, it was
"topical" and it had been successful in England and the
rest of Europe. MB became "available" after Nicholas
I, who "had forbidden its translation," was followed
in office by a more tolerant Alexander II in 1855.
"Above all, Mary Barton was original and distinctive.
It had made the novel as a vehicle for airing of current social evils respectable. For a new magazine, then,
it introduced a big new theme into Russian literature.
There had been nothing in Russian fiction before, of

either domestic or foreign origin, specifically about
the labour movement and its political struggle."

F. Dostoevsky wished to make his new publication
a success, in order to recapture his place in Russian
literary circles which he had lost when exiled to
Siberia ten years earlier. MB was, then, the choice
of a shrewd editor. But MB may have influence Crime
and Punishment. "What came to interest him in the period
leading up to the writing of Crime and Punishment was
the mass poverty of a big city. The questions which
had disturbed Dostoevsky at the beginning of his literary
career still disturbed him when he returned to literature, but he now saw them differently. Mary Barton
helped in forming this new viewpoint. In some way it
acted as a bridge between his old and new manner."
Similarities cited are, first, the "orthodox" Christian
stance from which the narrator criticizes Raskolnikov
and John Barton, second, the fact that both men act
as "dark, disturbing figures," third, that the structure
of both novels is alike in that characters are
grouped around a central figure, and fourth, the main
characters live in conditions of squalor which the
reader is made to see from the "inside."

160   Lane, Margaret. "Introduction" to Wives and Daughters.
          London: J.M. Dent & Sons; New York: E.P. Dutton
          & Co., pp. v-xiii. Everyman's Library, no. 110.
          Reprinted as "Mrs. Gaskell," in Lane, Purely for
          Pleasure. New York: Alfred A. Knopf, 1967,
          pp. 201-9. (See 305.)

"WD takes us at once into a vanished world, a
rural England before the days of railways and the
Industrial Revolution, and so into a climate of life
and modes of behaviour that in some aspects are as
strange to us as though they belonged to beings of
another planet. Yet, Mrs. Gaskell's tone of voice
is curiously modern" and her knowledge of people wide
and sophisticated.

161   McVeagh, John. "The Novels of Mrs. Gaskell." Unpub.
          Doc. Diss. (University of Birmingham).

(Not seen.)

162   Martin, Ernest William Lunn, ed. Country Life in
          England. London: Macdonald & Co.

(Not seen.)

163   Migdal, Seymour. "The Social Novel in Victorian England."
      DA 27, 2536A (University of California, Davis).
      EG pp. 46-94.

          "My aim is not to provide a detailed history of
      the Victorian social novel, but rather to explain each
      of the important works in the light of its intellectual
      and social milieu, and especially in the light of the
      didactic aims which the novelists set for themselves."

          MB is marred because EG in her Preface says she
      will deal with an "economic problem in other than
      economic terms," but she in fact bases the behavior
      of the characters solely on an interpretation of eco-
      nomic forces. "Sympathy" for her characters "means
      understanding what the workers feel" even if they are
      "obviously mistaken in their feelings." There is a
      split between "an economic interpretation of events
      and a religious-humanitarian one" borne out in the
      novel's conclusion when instead of introducing country
      values into the city EG translates her city characters
      to the country.

          NS, an advance over MB, is a book whose "propa-
      gandistic aims are generally the same . . . but the
      limitations of these aims are more openly expressed,
      mainly because the axioms of political economy are more
      openly expressed." Rather than achieving a marriage
      between equals at the end of the novel, Margaret Hale sub-
      mits to John Thornton's masculine strength. She moves
      much further toward him than he toward her. Margaret
      fits the pattern of "the innocent girl who wishes to
      be more humanitarian than the facts will allow . . . who
      gradually and painfully learns a superior knowledge."
      The novel adds "nothing"to this pattern.

164   Raff, Anton Donald. "Elizabeth Gaskell: A Critical
          Study." DA 28, 201A-02A (Cornell University).

          "I will examine her major fictions without placing
      undue emphasis, I hope, on her moral, social or religious
      ideals on the one hand, or on her charm, humor, pathos,
      and so forth on the other. . . . I wish to discover
      what their strengths and weaknesses are as works of
      art."

          In none of her works but C did EG write a "success-
      ful criticism of life." MB, R, and NS are marred by

ill-digested sociological ideas, SL contains several
of her "finest characters" but its ending sinks it,
and WD for all its artistry cannot compare in "intensity, originality, intellectual perspicacity and
subtlety, and moral penetration" with Vanity Fair and
Middlemarch.   "Mrs. Gaskell the artist had many
virtues but many limitations."

1967

165 Anon. "Yours Sincerely: Mrs. Gaskell in Full Plow,"
        TLS 16 Mar., 209-10.

        A favorable review of 157. In this review mention
is made of a letter EG wrote on the subject of the
Ruskin-Effie Grey marital difficulty.   The following
correspondence arose from it.

Lutyens, Mary.   "Mrs. Gaskell and Effie," TLS 23 Mar.,
        243.

        Refutes remarks about Effie Grey in 165.   EG was
eighteen years older than Effie.   There is no traceable
link between them, though they attended the same school,
Avonbank.   EG knew very little about Ruskin and Effie.
EG's letter to John Forster (Letters, pp. 286-89) on
the subject of their split, particularly that Effie
was engaged to some one else when she accepted Ruskin's
proposal, is "mischievous and damaging."

Kennedy, Malcolm D.   "Mrs. Gaskell," TLS 30 Mar., 267.

        Effie Grey was indeed engaged to someone else
when Ruskin proposed to her.   It was William McLeod,
Mr. Kennedy's maternal grandfather.

Lutyens, Mary.   "Mrs. Gaskell," TLS 6 Apr., 287.

        There is "no evidence" that Effie and William
McLeod were more to each other than dancing partners.

Kennedy, Malcolm D.   "Mrs. Gaskell," TLS 13 Apr., 309.

        Urges that Effie was jealous and upset when Mr.
McLeod subsequently married an Irish girl.

Dobbin, Andreena. "Mrs. Gaskell," <u>TLS</u> 20 Apr., 340.

    EG knew Scottish courting practices well and she
could easily be correct to believe that Effie indeed
had been engaged to William McLeod.

Lutyens, Mary. "Mrs. Gaskell," <u>TLS</u> 27 Apr., 368.

    Reasserts that Effie played the field, so to speak.
"I do not believe that Mr. Kennedy was ever in the
slightest danger of having Effie as a grandmother."

Kennedy, Malcolm D. "Mrs. Gaskell," <u>TLS</u> 4 May, 384.

    Kennedy is unpersuaded by Lutyens' assertion that
Effie would not be likely to make or break engagements
willy-nilly.

166   Chapple, J.A.V. "<u>North</u> and <u>South</u>: A Reassessment,"
      <u>Essays</u> <u>in</u> <u>Criticism</u> 17, 461-72. (See 182.)

    <u>NS</u> is a "far more tense and packed book" than <u>WD</u>
in part because exigencies of space in Dicken's <u>HW</u>
actually caused EG's novel to be compressed by Dickens'
editing. "The usual view of all this compression is
that <u>North</u> and <u>South</u> suffers artistically from being
huddled and hurried up at various points; but it could
be maintained that Mrs. Gaskell was, ironically, saved
from the full effects of one of her best qualities
[the "slow evolution and unhurried tempo" of her story-
telling]."

    "Despite the final title [the original was <u>Margaret</u>],
the union of North and South in the persons of Margaret
Hale and John Thornton is not for me the main point
of this novel. Nor is it the gradually achieved harmony
between masters and men in John Thornton's works. What
is, I think, at the heart of the book is the inner
progress of Margaret, culminating in that moment by
the ocean at Cromer [ch. 49]. If this is granted,
then most of the evident faults are no more than peri-
pheral. Its great strengths lie in the scrupulous
analyses, the full regard given to necessary distinctions,
and the elaborate interweaving of social and personal
themes."

167   Colby, Robert A. <u>Fiction</u> <u>With</u> <u>a</u> <u>Purpose</u>: <u>Major</u> <u>and</u>
      <u>Minor</u> <u>Nineteenth-Century</u> <u>Novels</u>. Bloomington

and London: Indiana University Press.

Ch. 7 "The Mill on the Floss: Maggie Tulliver
and the Child of Nature," pp. 213-55, contains several
references to MC, a story that influenced George
Eliot's novel.

168   Ellis, J.B.   "Mrs. Gaskell on the Continent," N&Q NS
        14 [212], 372-73.

Notes the existence of an 1857 Tauchnitz reprint
edition of LCB, which contains the text of the first
edition. No bibliography of EG lists or even suggests
that such an edition ever existed.

169   H., M.J.   "'Lizzie Leigh': A Bibliographical Inquiry,"
        The Manchester Review 11, 132-33.

A request for photocopies of certain pages from
the 1854 edition of Lizzie Leigh and other stories
prompted an inquiry into the question of the actual
date of publication of this volume, which has been
traditionally listed as 1855 and which was published
in 1855 not 1854. The error is traced to The English
Catalogue of Books, 1835-1863, published in 1864, which
"lists the work as being published in 1854, and has no
entry for an 1855 edition." No doubt this listing "is
the source of all later [incorrect] references to an
1854 edition."

170   Handley, Graham.   "Mrs. Gaskell's Reading: Some Notes
        on Echoes and Epigraphs in 'Mary Barton'," Durham
        University Journal NS 28, 131-38.

EG's usage of epigraphs in MB "tends to set up a
reverberating relevance in the text which adds immensely
to our enjoyment of the novel and to our critical
appraisal of it."

171   Kawamoto, Shizuko.   "North and South: A Victorian
        Pride and Prejudice." Tsuda Review no. 12 (Nov.),
        43-54.

Like Jane Austen's Pride and Prejudice NS is concerned with the question, "Who is a gentleman?" Darcy
and Elizabeth in the first proposal scene in Pride and
Prejudice clash over whether a "gentleman" is determined
by social status or by character. "If we take North

and South as the social document of admitting industrial
capitalists into the rank of gentlemen," we can see in
both novels the "resolidification of the gentry."

.72   Kay, Brian and James Knowles. "Where 'Jane Eyre' And
      'Mary Barton' Were Born," Brontë Society Transac-
      tions 15 (Part 77), 145-48.

      Charlotte Brontë "commenced Jane Eyre in . . .
      August of 1846" in lodgings (83 Boundary St.) in
      Manchester, where she had brought her father for an
      eye operation, about one-half a mile or ten minutes
      walk from 121 Upper Rumford Street, the house in which
      EG wrote MB. 121 Rumford St--"its stucco had almost
      perished, the tiny front lawn was unkempt and overgrown
      with weeds, but some trace of dignity and elegance
      still seemed to cling to the building"--still stands,
      though it is now numbered 95. It belongs to Manchester
      University but is slated for demolition. Recent
      photographs of both houses are included.

.73   Lane, Margaret. "Introduction" to Mary Barton, A Tale
      of Manchester Life. London: J.M. Dent & Sons
      Ltd; New York: E.P. Dutton, pp. v-x. Everyman's
      Library, no. 598. "Select Bibliography," p. xi.
      (See 245.)

      EG, "that misleadingly gentle figure of Victorian
      literature," surprises us in MB. "It has an unexpected
      topicality about it, a relationship to themes of violence
      and unrest with which our world is only too familiar."
      One may read it to learn what "the dark and also human
      side of the labour question was like," but the book is
      also a "drama" which "fulfils the prime demands of a
      good novel: it holds our interest from the start, it
      develops a logical action and resolves it, the characters
      live and grow and we believe in them."

      EG's "approach is feminine; she takes pains to
      tell the truth; she sees it not in terms of economic
      fact but from the point of view of the men and women
      who lived through it. She has caught their tone of
      speech." Although "accused" by some critics of being
      sentimental, her "lapses are rare." A second criticism
      of MB, that EG was "morbidly fond of a solemn deathbed"
      has been answered by Kathleen Tillotson, 99, who
      explains why death, as a subject for literature, was
      more suited to Victorian than to modern tastes.

      MB "is not, by enduring standards, a great novel,"

but its "simple moral and message" is relevant to us
today.

174 Lane, Margaret. "Introduction" to Ruth. London:
     J.M. Dent and Sons; New York: E.P. Dutton and
     Co., pp. v-xiii. Everyman's Library, no. 673.
     Reprinted as "Mrs. Gaskell and the Fallen Woman,"
     in Lane, Purely for Pleasure. New York: Alfred
     A. Knopf, 1967, to pp. 211-18. (See 285.)

     A modern reader, heir to the effects of the sexual
revolution, must have a lively and sympathetic imagination to fully appreciate the courage it took for EG
to publish R in 1853. As a story it far surpasses in
quality LL(1850) a dry run on the subject of seduction
and illegitimacy. R followed MB and C; in consequence,
EG's "creative powers had considerably developed, she
was approaching her maturity as a writer and confronted
her task with a mixture of anxiety and confidence."
While she challenged convention by making her heroine
"innocent" even in her seduction and by asserting that
she was noble and redeemable after committing her great
sin against society, she did quail finally and cause
her heroine to die. "It is a sentimental and unnecessary
flaw in the novel." If anything, "what revolts us"
in R is "the implacable cruelty and hypocrisy of an
age which in many ways seems so much less terrible,
so much more stable and comforting than our own."

175 Lucas, John. "Mrs. Gaskell and Brotherhood," Tradition
     and toleration in nineteenth-century fiction:
     Critical essays on some English and American
     novels. Edited by David Howard, John Lucas, John
     Goode. New York: Barnes & Noble, Inc., pp. 141-
     205.

     Examines MB, NS and several social-problem novels
to show that "the flaws inherent in the genre of the
social-problem novel are a direct result of the
novelists' failure to deal really honestly with the
social experiences" about which they write. When these
social experiences become too threatening or too complex the novelist tends to rely on conventional political attitudes to "bridge all imaginative lacunae."
He is, for all his good intentions, a victim of his
class. The novelist in "recommending the brotherhood
of united interests as a solution to social problems
and prime aid to a nation of single-minded purpose
frequently looks to be undermined by a guilty recognition that it is solely to the advantage of the

class that proposes it."

MB: This social-problem novel differs from
Kingsley's Alton Locke and Disraeli's Sybil because
EG "is not interested in the idea of brotherhood that
Kingsley half dared to believe existed, and which
Disraeli probably knew did not." Through John Barton
EG examined a "representative" working-class man in
the 1830's and '40's. The accuracy of her treatment
is attested to by two contemporary reviews of the
novel. But she succeeds in carrying her analysis of
"the denseness and bewildering complexity of the
industrial experience" just so far. She uses the
incident of the murder as a way to "simplify a complexity
which has become too terrific for her to accept con-
sciously." The murder provides "a neat pattern"
enabling her to distance herself from her central
character. Unfortunately, she reduces the problems of
class antagonism to "a matter of individual violence,
so that though the pattern itself is intendedly representative it is fashioned out of quite arbitrary
material."

NS: For most readers NS "achieves less" than
MB, most likely because EG championed both the north
and her own class, "two very obvious whipping-boys
of social conscience." She defends the north against
southern "prejudices" but in this she is over-zealous.
She errs both by making the values of the north "consistent with her middle class liberal sympathies" and
by betraying her "affection" for the north. Dickens,
in Hard Times, remains completely out of sympathy with
the values of the north; hence, EG's much more "intelligent" and "informed" examination of industrial society
no doubt contributed to Dickens' "annoyance" with NS.
In NS EG illuminated the middle class attitudes towards
work and culture, and it is "precisely this element
of awareness how identities are partly responses to the
social reality, of how work must oppose leisure, that
is missing from Hard Times." Missing also in Dickens'
novel are the "positive virtues that go with the belief
in work."

NS, however, fails in the same way as MB. EG
shows successfully "how personal relations are 'tainted'
by class considerations;" but she contradicts herself
when "she tries to show that this need not be so."
Her "tactic" is to attempt to reconcile classes by
describing the friendship between Thornton and Higgins.
By doing so she denies the "inevitability of the
'tainting' to which she draws our attention." This
"pattern of reconciliation intrudes into and mocks

[EG's] real imaginative strength."

By her nature EG could not take advantage of the material in NS for a "great tragedy." Reading it one is "inevitably struck by an awareness of how men ought to be forced apart in spite of their feelings for one another; that class interests have to wreck personal relations."

176 Rotner, Arnold Herbert. "Mrs. Gaskell's Art." DA
     29, 272A (University of Colorado).

"The purpose of this study is twofold: first, to demonstrate that there is a form common to Mrs. Gaskell's didactic novels and another form common to her art novels; second, to demonstrate that the art form is aesthetically superior to the didactic form. These two ideas are developed by subjecting the novels to the criteria of narration, plot structure, charac- terization, and tone." The study examines MB and R as "didactic," NS as "transitional," and SL and WD as "art" novels.

"The art form is aesthetically superior to the didactic for the following reasons. The exposition and authorial intrusions of the didactic form remove the reader from the action and prevent the dramatic immediacy typical of the art novels. Although the plot structure of both novel forms is built upon contrast, the two-world settings of the didactic novels results in a wrenching effect as the reader is jerked from one world to the other through the progression of the narrative, while there exists a smoother and more unified effect in the one-world setting of the plot structure of the art form novel." The "art characters" are more true to life.

177 Shapiro, Charles. "Mrs. Gaskell and 'The Severe Truth,'"
     in Minor British Novelists. Edited by Charles
     Alva Hoyt. With a Preface by Harry T. Moore.
     Carbondale and Edwardsville: Southern Illinois
     University Press, pp. 98-108. In the series
     Crosscurrents: Modern Critiques, Harry T. Moore,
     General Editor.

Taking its theme from CB's advice, in a letter to EG, to be "your own woman" and to respect "the severe Truth" as a literary artist, this article assesses EG's failure, in MB, and her success, in C, to write truthfully.

In MB, EG fails in several categories: "all the
characters who enter, speak, and disappear in the novel,
rich and poor alike, are frightful caricatures, gro-
tesques unredeemed by either artistry or wit;" "The
plot . . . is unbelievably forced and foolish." EG
fails to make the setting reflect character, she over-
uses the device of contrasting background with inhabi-
tants, in short, she sacrifices "all to get her fairly
simple messages across to her reader." The "best
portions" of MB, the portraits of the Carson women,
reflect EG's more characteristic literary self. This
self "carries over" into C, her "best work."

"Cranford, in a real sense, is Mrs. Gaskell, because
it is honest, observant, compassionate: and it is
her best work because it sees clearly and holds together
as an artistic creation. The tone is set right at the
outset, announcing themes, proclaiming affection, hinting
at soft criticisms. For though some critics see Cranford
as a collection of assorted tales and episodes united
by a common locale, it is very much a novel in the same
way that Winesburg, Ohio and The Dubliners are more than
short story collections."

In C, character portrayal, especially Miss Matty's,
is more effective, and "social criticism is sly and not,
as in Mary Barton, delivered with a drastic, heavy
hand." EG's "strength lies in how well she knows and
loves her characters and this, in turn, rests on her
femininity, her own qualities as a good woman."

EG and C both have "depths of a Freudian nature."
The women in C seem threatened by any mention of sex,
while the men "are either elderly and therefore non-
sexual or are confirmed in their active bachelorhood."
Miss Matty's brother, Peter, however, "ran away from
his parsonage home as a youth after a series of pranks,
some of which were of an obvious transvestite nature."
"This womanly world of Cranford does have its compli-
cations."

"Let us love Cranford and forgive her for the rest."

1968

78 Chapman, Raymond. The Victorian Debate: English
       Literature and Society 1832-1901. New York:
       Basic Books, Inc., Publishers, pp. 127ff. Litera-
       ture and Society, General Editor, Herbert Tint.

This survey of Victorian society attempts to bring

the reader into close contact with the Victorian mind.
EG figures in the category of the social novelist whose
intellectual equipment did not match the effectiveness
of her sympathetic power as a writer to portray suffering humanity. "There is a calm innocence in all
her books, the innocence of the child who utters profound truth in over-simplification." Yet the excellence of NS as a social novel cannot be denied. "There
is no work of the time that gives a better idea of the
conflict between rival interests or a clearer view
of the minutiae of life in an industrial town."

179   Chapple, J.A.V., ed, and intro. Life in Manchester.
         Manchester, England: The Lancashire and Cheshire
         Antiquarian Society.

         (Not seen.)

180   Handley, Graham. Sylvia's Lovers (Mrs. Gaskell).
         Oxford: Basil Blackwell. Notes on English Litera-
         ture, no. 24; Chief Advisor; John D. Jump; General
         Editor; W.H. Mason.

         A basic introduction to SL designed for "the school,
      college, and university student." Suggests that the
      "conventional" attitude to EG, perhaps best expressed
      by David Cecil, 28, no longer holds in the face of
      present understanding of EG. She was a "many-sided"
      woman who grew more deeply aware of the art of the
      novel and "of her own responsibilities as a writer."
      She never "ceased to 'learn' that people, in their
      independent and moving individuality, are what matter
      in fiction." SL, though uneven, is a story told "by
      a good, sometimes a superb story-teller." The novelist
      is still much "under-rated."

181   Harris, Wendell V. "English Short Fiction in the 19th
         Century," Studies in Short Fiction 6, 1-93. EG
         pp. 32-34.

         "Mrs. Gaskell's greatest claim on our interest
      . . . lies in Cranford . . . which though it has far
      more unity than a mere collection of stories about a
      single locale, is after all episodic and more truly
      belongs to the history of short fiction than some of
      her shorter pieces." EG's short stories "are interesting
      but in none does one find the economy and control Mrs.
      Gaskell exhibits in Cranford. The fact is as one
      would expect. Lacking the techniques for quickly and

economically sketching character and creating background
and atmosphere, Mrs. Gaskell, like the average writer
of the time, tended to see striking incident as the best
material for shorter fiction."

182   McVeagh, J.   "Notes on Mrs. Gaskell's Narrative Tech-
          nique," Essays in Criticism 18, 461-70.

          Contrary to J.A.V. Chapple's argument, 166, the
      compressed ending of NS was not satisfactory to EG
      herself nor is such compression typical of EG's best
      work. In fact, NS "is indeed a substantial novel but
      its ending is an accident, and untypical; the real
      substance is of a piece with the other stories, and is
      the outcome of cool leisurely contemplation and a
      narrative style utterly different from the panic cramming
      into which that novel collapses. How leisurely Mrs.
      Gaskell's art was has not been fully recognised even
      now."

          EG's real virtues result from her "theoretical
      unsoundness." "It is because Mrs. Gaskell was bad at
      organization that she was able to achieve the fineness
      which, here and there, transcends the ordinary and makes
      possible her most characteristic triumphs: contrast,
      irony, vividness, moral firmness--if and when she hits
      on a subject that suits her." EG "relied for her final
      effect time and time again on the crude accumulation
      of set scenes." "Another way of putting it would be
      that Mrs. Gaskell employs tableau-narrative. The main
      stages of the main action clear in her mind, she
      organises the novel as a series of dramatic episodes."

          EG is "less a novelist than a raconteur, and the
      amateurish nature of her talent has to be recognised
      as an integral part of her literary abilities in a
      final assessment of her status. This is why Mr. Chapple's
      praise of North and South falters, because the qualities
      he admires are not really Mrs. Gaskell's at all."

183   Martin, Hazel T. Petticoat Rebels: A Study of the
          Novels of Social Protest of George Eliot, Elizabeth
          Gaskell, and Charlotte Brontë. New York: Helios.

          (Not seen.)

184   Rayner, Dora Florence. "Mrs. Gaskell's North and South
          considered as a social novel and in relation to
          her development as an artist." Unpub. Doc. Diss.

(University of London).

A study of a much under-rated book encompassing
examinations into how literary and social contexts
shaped it, how the impact of Manchester and the
economic theory developed there is expressed in the
novel, how the book accommodated or answered criticism
of MB, and how NS reflects Carlyle's social theories.
NS is also compared to MB, an effort which entails
the examination of the composition of both works and
of the discernible changes that occur between MB and
NS. Other issues are EG's treatment of industrial
themes in other works, and an appraisal of R as a step-
ping stone in her development between MB and NS. Lastly,
NS is appraised as a work of art, as a vehicle for a
social message, and as a study in the development of
Margaret Hale's character. An appendix provides details
of the composition and publication of the novel.

185 Roberts, John K. "A Note on English Writers and Welsh
          Railways," The Anglo-Welsh Review 17, 136-38.

     "Mrs. Gaskell, in a short story, as early as 1850,
described the remote charm of Penmorpha precisely because
it was 'so different from the town and hamlets into which
the English throng in summer'." Awareness of Wales'
beauty made most Victorians of note regret modern
developments, symbolized by the railway, taking place
there.

186 Tarr, Rodger Lee. "Carlyle's Influence Upon The Mid-
          Victorian Social Novels of Gaskell, Kinglsey, And
          Dickens." DA 29, 2285A (University of South
          Carolina).

     In the three novelists studied "parallels" are
found "between Carlyle's concepts and those found in
the novels under consideration [that] are too particu-
larized and too significant to admit generalities."
The survey of Carlyle's attitude to the novel concludes:
"Of primary importance in his conception of the relative
value of extended prose fiction is his adamant conclusion that all worthwhile novels must include a purpose
wrought with intensity of conviction, which must be
supported by reality, truth, and belief."

     MB and NS are social novels, novels with a purpose.
Kathleen Tillotson, 99, is wrong when she "dismisses
too hastily the intent of the two novels, especially
in the light of Carlyle's conception of purpose and

message." "In both novels, she centers her message on
the Doctrine of Social Affection; in both novels, she
contends that money is not the answer to class relation;
and in both novels, she regards spiritual contemplation
and moral endeavor as prerequisites to social harmony."
The significant moments in the novels are seen to bear
this out: in MB the inartistic reconciliation between
John Barton and Mr. Carson; in NS, a more artistic
novel designed to examine the two nations of rich and
poor, in the bond achieved between Thornton the master
and Higgins the worker.

87 Tarratt, Margaret.   "Cranford and 'the Strict Code of
        Gentility,'" Essays in Criticism 18, 152-63.

        C, originally conceived as a brief article for a
magazine, "poses a problem for the critic since it is
not clear it has a 'structure' at all." This issue
is perceptively argued by Martin Dodsworth, 133, whose
"article is important in stressing the seriousness of
Elizabeth Gaskell's preoccupation and in its assertion
of thematic unity." But he underestimates "the extent
of the author's conscious control of her material."

        It is incorrect to say that Mrs. Gaskell meant
individuals to characterize social groups in C. "Martin
Dodsworth adopts Miss Deborah Jenkyns as the epitome
of the standards and responses of the Cranford ladies.
In many respects, however, Miss Jenkyns is an idiosyncratic personality rather than an archetypal figure."
"The identification of Miss Jenkyns with 'the strict
code of gentility' is crucial, since it enforces a
rigid limitation of the social milieu, founded on principles which she alone understands. It is on this
score and not that of aggressive feminism that she is
implicitly criticised." After Miss Jenkyns' death her
sister, Matty, and other Cranford ladies achieve more
human attitudes towards social conventions. "As far
as the situation [Dodsworth] describes in Cranford did
exist it derived from fear of self assertion in opposition to the conventions of society. It is not feminine
assertiveness but feminine subservience that is in
question."

88 Wolfe, Patricia A.   "Structure and Movement in Cranford,"
        Nineteenth Century Fiction 23, 161-76.

        Martin Dodsworth, 133, contributed much to an
understanding of C by "seeing a distinct movement in
the novel" and "in believing that this progression

advances from a complete rejection of the male at the
beginning of the book to a complete acceptance of him
at the end." He goes wrong, however, when he pictures
a male "defeat of Cranford ladies." The reintroduction
of male vitality into Cranford comes about "by the
emergence of genuine femininity as manifested in the
character of Miss Matty. The structure of the novel,
then, is based on characterization, not incident or
plot; and it is the females who dominate this element
of the book."

C is essentially a story in two parts, each governed
by a Jenkyns sister. After Deborah Jenkyns' death the
strict code of gentility she had instated in Cranford
is inherited by her sister, Miss Matty, a woman who
admires and emulates her sister as best she can. By
the novel's end, however, latent feminine qualities
emerge in Miss Matty.

"Four incidents at the center of the novel mirror
the progression of the book as a whole, and Miss Matty's
reaction to them gives the reader a clearer insight
into her psychological state. The magic show, the rob-
bery panic, the discovery of the magician, and the
subsequent generosity of the Cranford ladies serve to
hasten the development of both Matty and the town."

Miss Matty, in the course of the novel, "without
being aware of it . . . reshapes the values of her
society, and therein is the key to the novel's structure and movement. Not only does her good sense open
the minds of the female community to marriage, but also
to the idea of raising families."

By the end of the story Miss Matty stands independent, decisive and successful in her community "but
she . . . senses the ridiculousness of making this
strength a reason for pride in feminine superiority."
Dodsworth is not correct to see Miss Matty "pitiable"
because childless, nor to warn that the ending of C is
not a happy one. "To see her as essentially 'pitiable'
destroys the progress of the novel." "She found her
own salvation in selfless devotion to others and redeemed
Cranford by her example." "Can there be any doubt that
Miss Matty is meant to be honored rather than pitied?
Cranford is her story and her triumph."

1969

189 Brantlinger, Patrick. "The Case Against Trade Unions
         in Early Victorian Fiction," Victorian Studies 13,

37-52.

Early Victorian writers who expressed humanitarian ideas seldom exhibited "sympathy for trade unions and strikes." For example, in MB "the assassination of Harry Carson . . . is the work of John Barton the vindictive unionist rather than John Barton the frustrated Chartist." EG's own attitude to unions and strikes was shaped by the Glasgow spinners riot of 1837, where violence led to the death of a "nob," a substitute worker, and the practice of "oath-taking" was enjoined on the unionists. In MB John Barton takes an oath and then is chosen by lot to murder Harry Carson. "Barton's conscience is torn between allegiance to an oath which commands him to murder and his natural abhorrence of murder, and the oath wins." The murder does not seem to bother EG, given her sympathy for the working-class in MB, as much as does "the intimidation of the nobs" in her story. They are far more innocent victims of union vindictiveness than Harry Carson.

In NS "the idea of union tyranny includes the notion that strikes throw workers ill-able to afford it into involuntary unemployment." "Although Dickens deals with symbols [in Hard Times] while Mrs. Gaskell, with patient fidelity which is as fine as anything in fiction before 1855, deals with the details of reality, the problem posed by unionism in North and South is identical with that posed in Hard Times, and the solution is also identical--a rejection of the inhuman discipline of strikes and the loss of kindness which union enforcement entails." Yet EG sees the usefulness of a strike in NS and she can "partly agree" with Higgins, who believes that the union is necessary despite its defects. For EG the "union embodies the ideal of cooperation among individuals which is the antithesis of the ruthless competition practiced by masters," although the formation of unions has the tendency to set "class against class."

Despite EG's awareness of the futility of strikes to effect a rise in wages, her interest was with "moral" and "psychological" aspects of the conflict between masters and men in MB and NS. The "inadequacies of trade unionism" in these novels stem from "failures of human sympathy" not from "the law of wages."

"Despite the degeneration of the strike in North and South into violence, Mrs. Gaskell's tale of industrial pride and prejudice contains the most sympathetic account of trade union action in early Victorian fiction."

190 Ganz, Margaret. Elizabeth Gaskell: The Artist In
     Conflict. New York: Twayne Publishers, Inc.
     "Selected Bibliography," pp. 293-308, annotated.

     Rev. by K. Cushman in Library Journal 94, 2469;
by John Espey in Nineteenth Century Fiction 25 (1970),
121-26; by Edgar Wright in Victorian Studies 14 (1970),
97-98; by John McVeagh in Modern Language Review 65
(1970), 887-88.

     Reinterprets EG's life to show that "the oscil-
lation between artistic sophistication and conventional
reticence is at the heart of Mrs. Gaskell's undeniable
limitations as a writer; no true judgment of her nature
and of her achievement can be reached without concentrating on the conflict between her artistic impulses
and her committments to conventional standards of moral
and social behavior."

     MB, R, NS: In the three social novels, her "social
conscience" is hampered by "ambiguous feelings about
challenging the social order." She loses "objectivity"
when she sympathizes so deeply with John Barton's suffering. In NS she writes from a more "detached" point
of view, for her "muted emotional committment to the
deprived" permitted her to write more clearly about
masters. She was brought from "the sheer experience
of writing . . . Cranford to develop her latent powers
as a humorist and in Ruth to refine her descriptive
abilities and harness her narrative talents to the de-
vising of a cohernet plot" in NS. Because she was not
challenging the social order, which she had done to an
extent in R and MB, NS loses some of the power possessed
by the other works.

     MHC, C, WD: EG's true powers are revealed in the
more congenial atmosphere of domestic fiction. The
"humorist's vision" that emerges in MHC, C and WD
is in part an expression of her easiness with her
material. In WD her portraits of Cynthia Kirkpatrick
and Mrs. Gibson reveal EG's "transcendence of a rigid,
traditional conception of the nature of morality and
the purpose of art." She had learned to accept "human
complexities and . . . the need to do justice to these
with the freedom from didacticism which is the index
of the true artist. Humor was above all responsible
for that acceptance for it is to her humorous perception
of reality that she owed her nearest approach to an
emancipation from restrictive conventions. Humor's
mild iconoclasm provided the freedom which in turn
made her greatest artistry possible."

LCB, CP: Of the other works LCB is seen as a
reasonable performance given the conditions besetting
the biographer. The short stories reveal an aspect of
EG's psyche that is evident both in the didactic novels
and in her interest in abnormal states of mind. But
none of these short moral tales and tales of violence
can compare with the artistry of CP. The subject of
this story called forth EG's finest powers: "her
ability to describe nature feelingly, her skill in recording with an imagination the homely details of simple
but dedicated lives, and her insight into the basic
emotions and secret yearnings fostered by circumscribed
existence."

SL: This is a tragic tale which ranks with CP and
WD as one of her "outstanding achievements." "Yet,
despite the growth in 'technical control' and psychological maturity . . . its basic theme still reflects
those characteristic attitudes to general moral questions
and specific dilemmas of conscience" that mar MB, R
and, less so, NS.

91 Hindle, Alan. "New Editions," TLS 4 Dec., 1405.

A letter complaining that the editor of WD for
Penguin (see 192, 306) failed to include helpful notes:
no information is provided to explain EG's reference
to the Whitworth doctors. Did EG come across them
through "her friend and sponsor William Howitt, who
visited the Whitworth Doctors in 1818?"

92 Lerner, Laurence. "Introduction" to Wives and Daughters.
        Edited by Frank Glover Smith. Harmondsworth,
        England: Penguin Books Ltd, pp. 7-27. (See 306.)

WD, "the most neglected novel of its century,"
raises EG to the "level when we can compare her with
Jane Austen or George Eliot." WD "looks to Jane Austen,
the great writer of comedy, and forward to George Eliot,
the great writer of witty tragedy, and seems to bridge
the gap between them."

EG's own abilities lay more in the field of realistic writing where observant recording is required,
rather than in the writing of romance. "In all the
really memorable parts of Elizabeth Gaskell's fiction,
what we feel is the presence of an eye, an ear, and a
concern for truth: when romance creeps in, the power
goes. We need not conclude from this that realism is
superior to romance, but simply that her imagination was

essentially realistic. She had great gifts for rendering the world she knew and understood; but when
she tried to render the patterns of wish and fear, she
could fall back only on stereotypes."

193   Mews, Hazel. Frail Vessels: Woman's Role in Women's
        Novels from Fanny Burney to George Eliot. London:
        University of London, Athlone Press, p. 81 and
        passim.

        "Mrs. Gaskell's contribution to the analysis of
      the role of the Victorian woman was to extend the
      sympathy of her readers to the problems of working-
      class women and of 'fallen' women, and to interpret
      the challenge of the industrial development in the
      north, pointing out the significance it held for the
      women whose lives were affected by it, closely or re-
      motely. She was also the first to recognize the problems
      confronting the working educated woman in her new dual
      role, a role still much under discussion these hundred
      years after."

                              1970

194   Boyle, Patricia M. "Elizabeth C. Gaskell: Her Develop-
        ment and Achievement." DA 31, 5352A (University
        of Pennsylvania).

        "Mrs. Gaskell perhaps more than any other novelist
      of her period, represents in a quiet steady progressive
      way the processes at work shaping the development of
      the novel in the Victorian period." The study examines,
      also, the reasons why she remains a "minor novelist"
      and the ways in which she reflects and was influenced
      by critical theories of the novel at mid-century. EG,
      realizing that her use of "the reconciliation theme"
      in her early stories did not accord with the "demands
      of realism, an emerging school of fiction she identified
      herself with early in her career," changed her subject
      matter and altered her philosophical and ethical ideas
      between MB and WD. Although it "lacks artistry" MB
      deals with powerful moral problems which should be the
      material of a major novelist. As EG developed as an
      artist she retreated from controversial material. In
      WD "her finest novel . . . we find that Mrs. Gaskell
      has completely reversed the moral position implicit
      in her earliest works." In technique her method of
      psychological analysis in WD links her to the modern
      novelists.

95 Dodsworth, Martin. "Introduction" to North and South.
       Edited by Dorothy Collin. Harmondsworth, Eng.:
       Penguin Books Ltd., pp. 7-26. Penguin English
       Library. "Note on the Text," pp. 27-28. "Notes,"
       pp. 531-38. "Glossary of Dialect Words," pp.
       539-40. (See 288.)

     EG has been seen to comply with two orthodoxies:
first, the feminine writer stereotype of Cecil, 28,
which permits him to appreciate only four works, SL,
CP, WD and C; secondly, the reaction to it inspired by
Raymond Williams, 115, and John Lucas, 175, who examine
MB and NS as novels concerned with social problems.
One must enlarge the "terms of our second orthodoxy,"
however, to fully value EG's achievement in NS.

     EG looked to CB's novels for guidance in writing
NS, for both their concerns were with character. In
NS Margaret Hale must become aware of her passionate
sexual self before she can properly love an individual
person. The center of the novel turns upon the riot
scene in which Margaret instinctively moves to protect
John Thornton. EG's style seeks to mute the intensity
of passion underlying Margaret's action (particularly
if we compare her style to CB's), accomplishing at the
same time the submersion of the real forces at work
below the surface in a way that makes the scene not
overly alarming to readers. Her awareness of the unconscious sexual energy working within her characters
makes EG a forerunner of D.H. Lawrence.

96 Eddy, Spencer L., Jr. The Founding of "The Cornhill
       Magazine." Ball State Monograph Number Nineteen,
       Publications in English, No. 13. Muncie, Indiana:
       Ball States University, pp. 27-32.

     EG first became acquainted with George Smith,
publisher of Cornhill, when seeking materials for LCB.
CB's warm comments about Smith and "his full cooperation"
with the biography predisposed EG to turn to him as
a publisher when Dickens' editorial demands irked her.
But she did not readily publish in the Cornhill because
she disliked both Thackeray, its first editor, and
G.H. Lewes, who was to be on the magazine's staff.

     She did publish her short story, CT, in the second
issue of the Cornhill in February 1860. It is "a thin
and uncharacteristic piece." "Its slightness of humor
and bland subject-matter would not have offended the
most delicate of those 'ladies and children' Thackeray
hoped would be continually present at the Cornhill's

'social table,' but might not have entertained them
very much either." She later published WD "her best
work" in the Cornhill.

197 Gill, Stephen. Ed., and "Introduction" to Mary Barton,
     A Tale of Manchester Life. Harmondsworth, England:
     Penguin Books Ltd, pp. 9-28. The Penguin English
     Library. "Bibliography," pp. 29-30. "Prefatory
     Note on the Background to Mary Barton," pp. 31-32.
     "Appendix 1," EG's "first outline plan for the
     novel" which became MB, pp. 467-68. "Appendix 2,"
     text of EG's poem, "Sketches Among The Poor, No. 1,"
     pp. 469-72. "Notes," pp. 473-87. (See 246.)

     "Mrs Gaskell does not have the intense imagination
which could see in the fact of a disease an emblem of
essential truths about society. Neither does she have
the comprehensive, self-confident assertiveness of
Carlyle. She did however have one great advantage denied
to both Dickens and Carlyle, simply that she lived close
to what she described." While it is characteristic of
critics to praise EG's "truth to life" in her art "her
real strength is not fidelity to objects or scenes,
but fidelity to feelings." Her sensitivity "to individual response, in all its complexity" allows EG "to
rise above the mere exhibition of the 'naked sensibility'
[see 90] to convey a sense of the bigger movements
of which people like John Barton are a tiny part." "She
is able to grasp what are the sources of tension in a
society and to portray these imaginatively through the
filter of human emotions." For example, the character
of old Alice dramatizes the tension in industrial England
between town and country life. "In old Alice's longings
for the countryside," EG builds her sense of the contrast
of natural beauty and urban misery into an "evocation
of the sufferings of a whole generation early in the
most dynamic phase of the industrial revolution."

     MB has two weaknesses. The first springs from the
novel form, which requires a plot or story. EG's
strengths lay in "evocation, description [and] analysis
of a situation." No doubt she "willingly" acquiesced
to the "demands" of the novel convention when she
directed attention away from John Barton to Mary Barton.
The publisher only suggested the new title because
the story had already become Mary Barton's. EG, after
the murder, "progressively leads her reader out of the
real world of the 1840s into the world of romance, into,
that is, an altogether less demanding world."

     The second weakness rests in EG herself. She is

uncertain about her audience and subject because she
cannot resolve an inner conflict between her middle-
class values and her imaginative sympathy with the
position of the working-class. "As an imaginative
artist she is literally seeing more than she can finally
declare in her role as a mediator between the classes."
The murder scene in MB pinpoints both these weaknesses.
It fulfills the necessity for action and appears to be
a concession to the novel form. At the same time, she
at last abandons John Barton, a character for whom she
has up to this point betrayed the deepest sympathy.
Barton's early "hostility" to the employers is jus-
tifiable but when he becomes a murderer, he isolates
himself from all classes." His usefulness towards an
analysis of the industrial scene is at an end." By
the time she presents the reconciliation scene between
Carson and Barton the concerns of the novel have become
simplified. That EG should be brought to depict "so
unsatisfactory a scene" merely indicates the "problems"
faced by the novel in attempting to accommodate "not
just . . . persons and individual relationships, but
classes, movements, conflicts, [and] historical facts."

98 Gill, Stephen. "A Manuscript of Branwell Brontë, with
        Letters of Elizabeth Gaskell," Brontë Society
        Transactions 15 (part 80), 408-11.

        Prints the texts of two letters from EG to Jemima
Quillinan. The subject is the letter and the poem
Branwell Brontë sent to Wordsworth for his opinion
in 1837 (LCB, Ch. 8). EG printed the letter and what
she thought was the entire poem in LCB. In fact, the
poem she printed was incomplete but the entire poem has
now been recovered. The manuscript helps to make sense
of an otherwise meaningless poem which derives much
of its inspiration from Wordsworth's Ode: Intimations
of Immortality and from the evangelical hymns. "Branwell's vision, however, is much darker than Wordsworth's."

99 Hardy, Barbara. "Mrs Gaskell and George Eliot," in The
        Victorians. Edited by Arthur Pollard. London:
        Sphere Books, pp. 169-95. History of Literature
        in the English Language, Vol. 6. Brief annotated
        bibliography, p. 195.

        EG's "is a remarkable and various body of novels
and stories which have to be looked at in and for themselves." Her works reveal her as a novelist of unusual
individuality. "If I had to fix a label to her special
contribution to what we conveniently call 'The English

novel,' I would describe her as essentially a novelist of sensibility. It is a phrase which describes her changing powers throughout her career."

MB, NS: One observes a changing center of feeling in EG's "social" novels. MB is characterized by a powerful emotional appeal produced by our awareness of EG's own "bewildered and frustrated social questioning." Her ability to particularize the psychological make-up of her characters and to place them in a social context is already evident, and counterbalances the excessive morbidity in the book. Owing to the restraint of convention, Ruth, a character invested with considerable sensibility, remains psychologically incomplete. In NS EG succeeded not just in moving us by the "poignancy" of her own power of feeling. In NS she creates two centers of feeling in Margaret Hale and John Thornton. "We are moved and held not just by the dramatic liveliness, but by what it reveals of human nature." In NS we have present before us a "dramatized sensibility." "At last her novel of sensibility is both balanced and complete."

C: This story reveals "considerable complexity and subtlety in the presentation of feeling" but it stands apart from the other novels because of its "displaced personal centre." By piecing together the story of Miss Matty, "the true active centre," what at first appears to be "episodic sketches" becomes a story having "a very cunning continuity, quality and power to move."

CP, SL, WD: Like C, these works are "full of psychological variety." SL is EG's "greatest novel" because the play of passions between Sylvia and Philip are so finely drawn. SL and WD "are both two of the most moving, emotionally complex and morally tolerant studies of human strength and weakness in the English novel."

200 Lane, Margaret. "Introduction" to Cousin Phillis; My Lady Ludlow; Half A Life-Time Ago; Right at Last. London: J.M. Dent & Sons, Ltd; New York: E.P. Dutton & Co., Inc., pp. v-xv. Everyman's Library, no. 615. (See 301.)

Much of the introduction is devoted to CP. In CP EG "has worked on a subtler level than we imagined."

201 McVeagh, John. Elizabeth Gaskell. London: Routledge & Kegan Paul; New York: Humanities Press. The

Profiles in Literature Series; General Editor:
B.C. Southam.

A study for the modern reader designed as a "practical form of introduction" to the versatility and
"essential unity" of EG's work. Short selections are
taken from EG's three kinds of writing: the "novels
of social criticism," biography and "novels of country
life." Usually, each selection is preceded by an
introductory paragraph and followed by a paragraph of
analysis. It is the author's aim to show "the underlying
themes, attitudes and judgements of the various stories
. . . dealt with, indicating the essential unity of Mrs.
Gaskell's work."

In the book's last section "Limitations and
Achievement," emphasis falls on EG's "many-sided skill"
as a writer. Critics of her work often fail "to inte-
grate and harmonize her varied achievements." As a
result, her "versatility" has worked against her. To
set matters aright, it should not be insisted on that her
"works are the same; they are not, and there is certainly a duality [between her sociological talents and
comedic powers] in Mrs. Gaskell's total oeuvre which
remains when the parallels have been admitted. But if
the unifying qualities are noted first and seen to
underlie most of what she wrote, the idea that her
'true' genius was such-and-such a part of her character
and that it was misled into the wrong paths in this or
that group of stories--which therefore are to be re-
gretted as 'untrue'--will disappear. Instead the variety
will be recognized as a sign of the resilience and
versatility of her art."

Perhaps her "outstanding single quality" is the
"exceptional vividness of her pages." Since she "aimed
at an imitation of life that would be consistent and
unspoiled enough to rival the vitality of life itself"
she tended as an artist "to efface herself" from the
scenes she drew. For EG this was a conscious artistic
effort which saw its finest achievement in WD, in which
she combined "meaning with entertainment by keeping
the comedy brimming over, yet never degenerating into
farce, and by keeping the point there, always open to
view, yet eschewing moral reflection."

EG's weakest point can be seen in the "intellectual
confusion" in the moral pattern of a novel like SL.
"When she tries to draw a moral or force a meaning she
fails, for she lacks the mental stamina and the hard
core of rational power which are needed for that kind
of art."

202   McVeagh, John.   "The Making of 'Sylvia's Lovers',"
        Modern Language Review 65, 272-81.

        The answer to "what went wrong with Sylvia's Lovers"
        can be seen by tracing through her Letters, 157, which
        reveal that EG waited too long to complete her novel.
        Internal doubts and external obligations encouraged
        her to resort to "incident" to complete the third
        volume instead of continuing "the patient narrative
        of character conflict of the earlier two volumes."

203   Schwartz, Stephen Lee.   "Elizabeth Gaskell: The Novelist
        As Artist."   DA 132, 3269A (University of Rochester).

        Provides an analysis and summary of the bases of
        EG's critical reputation from 1900 to the present,
        interprets six of her novels, MB, C, R, NS, SL, WD,
        and evalutes "her artistic accomplishment."

        MB is "flawed by separation in style."   Tone in
        C actually shapes an episodic work into a subtle unity.
        R is "completely didactic" and the "least readable of
        her novels."   The structure of NS is "somewhat con-
        fused," because her central character's emotional growth
        does not really unite with her major concern, in this
        "panoramic novel," with "social and economic problems."
        SL is a failure, albeit an impressive one, owing to
        its "powerful" if finally "unconvincing characterization
        of Philip and Sylvia."   WD lacks "sustained interest."
        It is concluded that EG deserves no higher place in
        critical esteem than that she has been assigned.

204   Sharps, John Geoffrey.   Mrs. Gaskell's Observation And
        Invention: A Study of Her Non-Biographical
        Works.   With a Foreword by A. Stanton Whitfield.
        Fontwell, Sussex: Linden Press, distributed by
        Centaur Press, Ltd., 1970.

        Rev. by John R. Townsend in Guardian 9 Dec., 8.
        in British Book News Feb. (1971), 149; in Brontë Society
        Transactions 16 (1971), 55-56; in Times Educational
        Supplement 6 Aug. (1971), 13, 3 Sept. (1971), 20, and
        1 Oct. (1971), 26; by Graham Handley in N&Q NS 19 [217]
        (1972), 280; by Lawrence Jones in Victorian Studies 15
        (1972), 497-99; in Univ. of Edinburgh Journal 25
        (1972), 270.

        Discusses EG's non-biographical works in chrono-
        logical order, bringing relevant biographical infor-
        mation to bear upon the discussion of composition and

intention in her work. "To attempt a narrow definition
of our key-words, 'observation' and 'invention', appears
an unprofitable task; whatever meaning these terms have
when applied to the works of Mrs. Gaskell should emerge
from a detailed consideration, in order of publication,
of all her non-biographic writings--which is the method
here employed." "To sum up, Mrs. Gaskell sought to
observe what she had invented, and what she had invented
owed much to prior observations."

    Contains a wealth of information on a variety of
subjects. "Bibliographical Preliminaries And Comments
On The Chapple-Pollard Edition of Mrs. Gaskell's Letters,"
pp. xv-xxv. "Appendix I: The Genesis of Mary Barton,"
pp. 551-62, includes a copy of a "rough sketch" EG
made before starting to write MB. "Appendix II: The
Plot of North and South," pp. 563-74, contains an
analysis of the "difference between the way Charles
Dickens proposed the first part of the novel should be
serialized and how it eventually appeared in Household
Words." "Appendix III: The Ironical Origin of The
Life of Charlotte Brontë," pp. 575-78. "Appendix IV:
The Composition And Publication Of A Dark Night's Work,"
pp. 579-85. "Appendix V: The First Two Editions Of
Sylvia's Lovers," pp. 587-92. "Appendix VI: 'Night
Fancies,'" pp. 593-95, prints and discusses a short
poem attributed to EG by Chapple and Pollard in Appendix
F of the Letters, 157. It is not EG's. "Appendix VII:
Names Of Characters In Mrs. Gaskell's Fiction," pp.
597-603, indexes "every name belonging to a fictional
personage or to a historical personage not easily recognized as such." "Appendix VIII: Untraced Or Dubious
Gaskell Publications," pp. 605-12. "Bibliography,"
pp. 613-60. "Holders of Gaskell Manuscripts," pp. 661-
83. "Manuscripts Quoted or Cited in Printed Works,"
pp. 684-88. "Index From Mrs. Gaskell's Writings,"
pp. 689-93, including "Projected Works and Attributions,
Excluding Collective Editions and Editions of Her
Letters."

205 Tannacito, Dan John. "Transformal Structures: Anatomy
        Romance And Novelistic Romance As Prose Fictional
        Genres." DA 33, 5144A (University of Oregon).

    "This dissertation has two purposes, to contribute
to the poetics or prose fiction a comprehensible account
of a specific and generally unrecognized literary genre,
the anatomy-romance, and to show the similarity and
difference between this genre and the novelistic romance.
The initial chapter establishes a workable conception
of these genres as special kinds of structures on the

basis of Northrop Frye's prior treatment of these
genres and other related concepts in Anatomy of
Criticism."

In MB "the contrast between the novelistic aspect
and the aspect of romance of the work stems from the
difference between Gaskell's observation of an actual
society and her insistence on the way it could possibly
be. We might call the change from one aspect to another
and the concomitant shift in focus from John Barton to
Mary Barton a progressive kind of relation between the
novelistic plot and setting . . . and the romance
action and scene. This notion would capture Gaskell's
attempt to show a mimetic representation of the opposition between Barton and the manufacturer and then to
display the similarity of both in opposition to the
romance action and values."

206 Stowell, Helen Elizabeth. Quill Pens and Petticoats:
     a portrait of women of letters. London: Wayland
     Publishers Ltd.

     (Not seen.)

                          1971

207 Brewster, Jack. "The Virtuous Heroes in the English
     Novel." DA 32, 4601-2A (Indiana University).

     Examines eight heroes, Sir Charles Grandison, George
Knightley in Emma, John Thornton in NS, Thackeray's
Henry Esmond, George Eliot's Adam Bede and Daniel
Deronda, and Hardy's Gabriel Oak in Far From The Madding
Crowd, who form a class of sorts because their "distinguishing mark" is that by living within a "clear and
decisive moral code," given them by their authors, they
eventually achieve both "personal and social success."
"The primary characteristic of a virtuous hero is
internal equilibrium," which means that such a character
"accepts a standard of good conduct and lives by it."
When such a hero does not accept the author's "value
system" from the start of the novel--John Thornton and
Adam Bede do not--it is simply that the "codes they
start with" are incomplete and through the course of
the novel are "expanded . . . until they embrace all
the major values in the author's system." Thornton,
odious at the start of the novel because isolated and
ignorant of his workers' suffering, is "finally redeemed
because he renounces his isolationist attitude and changes
his policies as soon as he learns about the conditions

his workers really are in."

NS marks an advance over MB, a book in which EG
presented only "a diagram of reconciliation" between
Carson and Barton. After beginning NS she discovered
the potential for a virtuous hero in the society of the
industrial North and changed the title from "Margaret
Hale" to NS to "encompass the entire industrial society
in her vision." The novel form permits her to particularize Carlyle's abstract ideas. She does not elevate
her material by over-writing. The moment when Thornton
dines with his workers is not elevated with "symbolism"
though it is a remarkable moment in a book in which
"more is at stake . . . than in any other novel in
the dissertation."

208 Collin, Dorothy W. "The Composition of Mrs. Gaskell's
       North and South," Bulletin of the John Rylands
       Library Manchester 54, 67-93.

       Recounts, by examining the exchange of letters
among Dickens, EG and Dickens' sub-editor William Henry
Wills, the progress and frustrations involved in the
publication of NS. Included are the comparison of
Dickens' divisions of the manuscript versus EG's own
and an account of EG's method of expanding the novel
for publication as a bound edition. Gives a fuller but
not substantially different account from 57.

209 Easson, Angus. "Sources of the Following from Mrs.
       Gaskell's 'North and South' (1854-5)," N&Q NS 18
       [216], 263-64.

       Request for sources of particular passages in NS.

     Shipps, Anthony W. "Sources of the Following from
       Mrs. Gaskell's 'North and South' (1854-5)," N&Q
       NS 18 [216] (Nov. 1971), 424.

       Gives references for one of sources sought in
Easson's request.

210 Gérin, Winifred, ed., and intro. The Life of Charlotte
       Brontë. London: Folio Society.

       (Not seen.)

211 McCready, H.W. "Elizabeth Gaskell and the cotton
       famine in Manchester: some unpublished letters,"
       Historic Society of Lancashire and Cheshire Trans-
       actions 123, 144-50.

     (Not seen.)

212 Messinger, Gary Steven. "Visions of Manchester: A
       Study of the Role of Urban Imagery in History,
       1780-1878." Unpub. Doc. Diss. (Harvard University).

     The responses of Disraeli, EG and Dickens to the
     urban industrial phenomenon of Manchester are discussed
     at length.

          EG saw in MB an "opportunity" to show "little-known
     details of Manchester life." Her "argument" is that
     "the system of life in Manchester forces tragedy upon
     fundamentally decent people. One's predominant emotions
     at the end of the book are sympathy and pessimism.
     The persona of the authoress is that of a nurse who
     sees no final remedy for the sorrow she witnesses daily,
     but who stresses the importance of bearing with the suf-
     ferers nonetheless." But the only answer she offers
     to the situation is "escape." The reader comes closest
     to EG's own attitudes and philosophy in the pronounce-
     ments of Job Legh.

          In NS EG's "change in attitude [is] more a matter
     of emphasis than doctrine." Part of the change was
     inspired by her friendship with James Nasmyth, "inventor
     of the steam hammer and one of the more kind-hearted
     Manchester manufacturers." The theme of NS permits
     EG to explore opposites, especially the relative merits
     of country versus city life. This "exploration ultimately
     ends in ambivalence" which the author does not resolve.
     "As the novel ends, their [John and Margaret Hale
     Thornton] future place of residence is left unspecified."

          It is clear, however, that the writers discussed
     avoid a "rigorously factual approach." "Although the
     novelists serve as valuable and at times unique sources
     of information about the mores of Manchester citizens,
     they all fail to convey any extensive understanding
     of the actual complexity of the urban society being
     discussed." "For example, one sees no acknowledgement
     in their works that narrow minded millowners were really
     more characteristic of the small factory towns surrounding
     Manchester than of Manchester itself; no mention of the
     difference in outlook between merchants and manufacturers;
     no acknowledgement of the various urban relief agencies

which had appeared in the town as far back as the 1830's;
no sense for the exact proportion of workers (were they
even a majority?) who advocated violent responses to
social problems; no information about the successes
and failures of the educational institutes which workers
had themselves established for their own aid; and no
discussion of the possibility that at least a few of
the difficulties in the newly urbanized environment
might simply have been holdovers from the less urbanized
ways of life of earlier eras or other places."

Because these writers disguised Manchester or
aggregated various places along with Manchester to
make their "Coketown," "Mowbray," or "Milton," many
distinctions within English society were lost. "In a
powerful but actually rather vague way the reader thus
obtained the feeling that Manchester was an archetype
for all of English society."

In yet another way the novelists introduced anach-
ronisms into their books. EG shared this tendency by
setting MB years before the date it was published. Such
a practice blurred historical accuracy.

These novels about Manchester were "fantastic best
sellers." But the importance of Manchester was not
mainly literary, as London was. The novelists "sensed
and eloquently expressed the less logical aspects of a
mood--a shared curiosity which was evident along an
entire spectrum of investigative responses."

213 Page, Norman. "'Ruth' and 'Hard Times': A Dickens
        Source," N&Q NS 18 [216], 413.

        "All in all, however, it seems clear that Hard
Times would not be quite the novel it is if Dickens had
not read Ruth."

214 Thomas, L.H.C., "Germany, German Literature and
        Nineteenth-Century British Novelists," in affinities:
        Essays in German and English Literature. Edited
        by R.W. Last. London: Oswald Wolff Ltd., pp.
        34-51. EG pp. 46-47.

        Points out German allusions in MB, C, and NS.

215 Weiland, Steven. "Chartism and English Literature
        1838-1850." Unpub. Doc. Diss. (University of
        Chicago). EG pp. 57-75.

Ch. 2 "Chartism And The Novel," pp. 17-112, discusses novels by six authors: Frances Trollope's <u>Michael Armstrong</u> <u>The</u> <u>Factory</u> <u>Boy</u>(1840), Charlotte Elizabeth Tonna's <u>Helen</u> <u>Fleetwood</u>(1841), Dickens' <u>Barnaby</u> <u>Rudge</u> (1841), Disraeli's <u>Sybil</u>(1845), EG's <u>MB</u>(1848), and Kingsley's <u>Alton</u> <u>Locke</u>(1850). Of the six, EG is shown to have best understood the causes of Chartism and to be the most comprehensive in her reactions to it. Through the character of John Barton EG praises the basic idealism that spurred the Chartist movement. She was aware of the potential for violence among Chartists and depicts violence in her novel. Yet John Barton's act of murder is given a long and sympathetic history, and part of the responsibility for it, she argues, must be placed with the masters. She did not advocate violence, but rather reconciliation between the working class and the middle class. Her stance was actually quite contemporary, for even radical Chartists, by 1848, had realized the need to alter the adversary nature of Chartist political tactics. But reconciliation was not to be easily achieved. She presents the working class as an effective and distinct entity, independent of the middle class. She does this by upholding at least two tenets of Chartism, that the source of all value is labor and that the masters mistreat their workers and rob them of their just reward. At the same time she urges that the classes are interdependent and envisions a reconciliation between classes echoing the conventional teaching of Political Economy that manufacturers and workers must necessarily work together for the benefit of both.

1972

216 Franko, Patricia. "The Emergence of Harmony: Development in the Novels of Mrs. Gaskell." <u>DA</u> 34, 769A (Temple University).

EG's religious training and active sympathies prepared her, as an artist, to seek to reconcile opposites she observed both within and without herself. "As an artist, Mrs. Gaskell was forced to rise above any inner conflict which threatened to sap her energy. For her, the unity of God, the First Creative Force, was reflected to some degree in the unity of the artist. She felt that a writer had to be capable of bringing all that he was to the act of creation if he were to create anything of value. In Mrs. Gaskell's opinion, a novel was the sum total of its author's experience spontaneously transformed into a fictional world through his ability to empathize wholeheartedly with the imaginary characters who peopled that world."

Because she would not deny the fact of inner conflict her novels were "structured around a basic Victorian antithesis." MB deals with "the paradox of
creativity and destruction in nineteenth-century
industrialization;" R "dramatizes the problem of self-
hood versus selfishness;" C "explores the relative
merits of feminism and femininity;" NS "emphasizes the
struggle for permanence in a world of change;" SL "demon-
strates the tension between romance and reality;" and
WD "crystallizes the conflict between convention and
the individual." Given the presence of conflicting
opposites in society "the body of Mrs. Gaskell's work
becomes a dialectic whose end is the successful formulation of a cohesive vision of reality."

17 Murray, Philip. "Fantasia On A Theme by Mrs. Gaskell,"
    Poetry 120, 228-29.

    A poem inspired by Cranford.

18 Butler, Marilyn. "The Uniqueness of Cynthia Kirkpatrick:
    Elizabeth Gaskell's Wives and Daughters and Maria
    Edgeworth's Helen," Review of English Studies NS
    23, 278-90.

    Argues that, while the plot for WD was taken from
    Fredrika Bremer's A Diary, the character of Cynthia
    Kirkpatrick was inspired by the character of Cecelia
    in Maria Edgeworth's Helen.

    "What, finally, of Cynthia Kirkpatrick? Is she
    a creation worthy of a greater novelist than Mrs.
    Gaskell generally proved herself to be? The more remote
    standpoint which Mrs. Gaskell adopts in relation to her
    character (even if inspired, as I have suggested, by
    a desire to prevent her from stealing the limelight
    from Molly) makes a fascinating figure out of Cynthia,
    more fascinating, because more inscrutable, than Maria
    Edgeworth's Cecelia. But if the two novelists are
    compared in terms of their handling of the central
    characters in relation to one another, and in relation
    to a theme, it appears to be Maria Edgeworth rather
    than Mrs. Gaskell who deserves much of the praise which
    has been bestowed on Wives and Daughters."

219 Smith, David. "Mary Barton and Hard Times: Their Social
    Insights," Mosaic 5, 97-112.

"Where Mary Barton presents a defiant, and then
chastened, working class leader, Hard Times shows us
the hegemony that a dehumanising ideology has assumed
root and branch over British society, and it contains
within it an implicit demand for a counter-culture.
In all sorts of ways unknown to Dickens, the counter-
culture had already begun its struggle."

220   Spachs, Patricia Meyer. "Taking Care: Some Women
         Novelists," Novel 6, 36-51.

         Lacking Jane Austen's "capacity for irony," wit,
"lightness of tone" and "economy of touch," EG never-
theless possesses a "special" quality: "a steady
integrity of observation which creates the sense of
penetrating accuracy." In MB and NS she "treats female
dilemmas" under the guise of larger social issues:
relationships between masters and men. "Hidden analogies
between the plight of women and of workmen surge beneath
the surface, never quite explicit." But in WD, where
she avoids the industrial scene, she shows an awareness
of "what it is men do with their time." "The contrast
between necessary male occupations and unnecessary
female ones, hinted in Jane Austen, is developed in Wives
and Daughters; it forms the novel's perspective on
female problems."

         Since nothing can alter the fact that a woman's
occupation is established by "fate," "what takes its
place as a feminine preoccupation" in WD "is the issue
of how one should deal with feeling." The heroine,
Molly Gibson, has several "models" available to her
in the novel. In some ways WD is more effective because
"unfinished." One assumes that Molly will marry Roger
Hamely in the last chapter but "despite the romanti-
cism of her plot, Mrs. Gaskell has managed to pursue
a searching investigation of the feminine situation."
It is not at all apparent what the answers are to the
dilemmas she reveals.

221   Watson, Elizabeth Porges. Ed., and "Introduction" to
         Cranford. London: Oxford University Press, pp.
         vii-xii. Oxford English Novels; General Editor,
         James Kinsley. "Select Bibliography," pp. xv-
         xvi. "A Chronology of Elizabeth Gaskell," pp.
         xvii-xix. "Appendix: Reprint of "The Last Gene-
         ration in England," (1849), pp. 161-178. "Revisions
         of the Text of Cranford," pp. 179-83. "Explanatory
         Notes," pp. 185-200. (See 284.)

A "dichotomy" exists in EG which a line from C
best describes: "I had vibrated all my life between
Drumble [Manchester] and Cranford [Knutsford]." Having
lived in Knutsford EG "retained . . . a deep affection
for a particular pattern of existence, and a deeper
trust in the values which sustained it." After MB
she underwent an "imaginative reaction" which found
her in "The Last Generation in England" (prototype for
C) and in MHC working up into artistic form her sense
of the relation of present to past. In these two works
EG developed her narrative stance for C. Mary Smith,
the narrator in C, "is for Mrs. Gaskell the perfect
medium of presentation; subjective in her viewpoint
by virtue of up-bringing and familiarity, and objective
by virtue of her age (she is from the beginning clearly
much younger than the other characters) and by some
diversity of experience."

The "structure" of C "is based on the play of
time, of the contact of the past, through memory, by
accident, or by association with the present." The
submerged Cranford values appear dramatically at the
"center" of the story when Miss Matty exchanges her
money for the poor man's worthless banknote in Mr.
Johnson's shop. Though the ending was not foreseen
when EG began C, it reinforces the pattern of experience in which reminiscence and the past may irrupt in
a concrete and affirmative way, causing the greatest
joy. Her lost brother Peter's return to Cranford "gives
to the climax of the story that quality which J.R.R.
Tolkien in his Essay on Fairystories has called
Eucatastrophic, the happy ending that gives 'a fleeting
glimpse of joy, beyond the walls of the world, poignant
as grief.'"

1973

222 Axe, Kathryn. "Elizabeth Cleghorn Gaskell: A Critical
        Evaluation of Her Novels." Unpub. Doc. Diss.
        (University of Kansas).

     (Not seen.)

223 Easson, Angus. Ed., and "Introduction" to North and
        South. London, New York: Oxford University
        Press, pp. ix-xviii. Oxford English Novels;
        General Editor: James Kinsley. "Select Biblio-
        graphy," pp. xxi-xxii. "A Chronology of Elizabeth
        Gaskell," pp. xxiii-xxv. (See 289.)

Compares NS to Dickens' Hard Times, concluding
that while EG does not have "the successes of Dickens"
she "raises questions, leaving us finally with the
feeling that they have been explored, and left unanswered
only because she is aware of the complexity of the
situation she has created." NS is the more "satisfactory" novel "because it works more consistently
on this plane of psychological drama." NS shows, as
well, an advance beyond MB. "North and South in its
treatment of social themes is far more balanced than
Mary Barton, indeed insists upon the debate, and finds
no facile solution, such as there had been in Carson's
conversion and reconciliation at John Barton's death-
bed. The novel is open-ended in this respect; Thornton
is a good master, Higgins a good worker, and so they
can co-operate. We are aware though that there are
bad of both; it is a realism set against the formalism
of the roles in Hard Times." The critics' stress of
the "roles of Margaret and Thornton is . . . right,
for . . . it is their tentative approaches and their
reconciliation in love that make North and South a
great novel."

224   Furbank, P.N.   "Mendacity in Mrs. Gaskell," Encounter
        40 no. 6, 51-55.

Analyzes EG's narrative stance in NS. The physical
transcriptions" of Margaret Hale's "emotional reactions"
are given to us in "a curious and special 'heroine'
style." EG confuses the reader at times because "it
is often difficult to tell who is supposed to be
noticing Margaret's emotional reactions. Confusion
arises from the fact that while "she pretends to be
writing 'from the outside,' she is 'really writing
from the inside.'" "There is no reason why this should
be a bad method. In fact it is a very interesting one;
only an author who uses it has a particular need to
play fair, and I do not think that Mrs Gaskell does so."

In NS one is struck by "the excessive and painful
self-consciousness of the heroine," who must always
be ready to face any "social challenge." "And to follow
all her physical symptoms is to watch her facing these
challenges." In both NS and C EG shows she "is the
poet of deceit; she knows that country of shams better
than anyone. Only the trouble is, Miss Matty seems
to have taken a hand in writing North and South."

225   Gorsky, Susan R.   "Old Maids and New Women: Alter-
        natives to Marriage in Englishwomen's Novels,

1847-1915," Journal of Popular Culture 7, 68-85.

Surveys the changing attitudes of fictional female
characters toward marriage. Miss Matty Jenkyns in C
provides an example of this change. She remains unmarried "not through choice but through necessity."
But, unlike the modern "new woman," Marion Vincent
in Mrs. Ward's Testing of Diana Mallory (1908), "Matty
would have married if she could have while Marion
rejects a suitable proposal on personal and ethical
grounds."

226   Palmer, Helen H., and Anne Jane Dyson. English Novel
          Explication: Criticism to 1972. Hamden, Connec-
          ticut: Shoe String Press, Inc., pp. 117-19.

This compilation is meant to supplement and con-
tinue the work of Bell and Baird, The English Novel
1578-1956, 106, by providing coverage of twentieth
century criticisms from 1958 to 1972. Includes a "List
of Books Indexed," pp. 277-304, and a "List of Journals
Indexed," pp. 305-18.

227   Panuska, J. "Character Artistry in the Novels of
          E.C. Gaskell." Unpub. Doc. Diss. (University of
          Alberta).

(Not seen.)

228   Willens, Susan Popkins. "The Novels of Elizabeth
          Gaskell: The Comic Vision." DA 33, 6889A (Catholic
          University of America). "Appendix 1: Narrative
          Control of Time in Sylvia's Lovers," pp. 222-26.
          "Appendix 2: Quantities in Installments of Wives
          and Daughters," pp. 227-28. "Appendix 3: Compari-
          son of Past and Present in Wives and Daughters,"
          pp. 229-32.

This study "builds upon Wright's [see 155] observation of Mrs. Gaskell's novels," because he rightly
observes that EG is "a social novelist." But the study
offers "a new look" at the six major novels, all of which
"share the comic vision" because all affirm that "reality
[is] meaningful and redemptive." All of her novels
deal with the "impact of change on a stable society."
As EG developed as an artist she employed different
literary traditions and genres--romance, pastoral,
historical novel--in her books, and she resolutely
adhered to the form (three volume, etc.) in which the

work was to be published.

    A shift from realism to romance occurs in MB
revealing a "tension between convservative values and
sympathy for those who suffer from the emerging industrial system." This shift suggests the "artist in
conflict" depicted by Margaret Ganz, 190. R is a
"romance" written in the "same mode of presentation as
Hawthorne's The Scarlet Letter." The setting and description "are all psychological placements revealing the
heroine's state at the time," except when, in the
third volume, "the public volume," almost all description disappears. C depends upon the pastoral tradition
in which "an idealized village is contrasted with the
city in order to dramatize the conservative, humane
values of village life." NS is "a success second only
to WD" in dealing with quantities of material. In NS
she does not "merely equate values," she evaluates
"several modes of life dramatized toward a reconciliation
of values." SL derives from Scott's formulation of the
"historical novel." WD is a "summary and conclusion
of all her work."

                              1974

229 Basch, Françoise. Relative Creatures: Victorian Women
     in Society and the Novel 1837-67. Translated by
     Anthony Rudolph. London: Allen Lane, Penguin
     Books Ltd. Short "Bibliography," pp. 327-28.

    A study broken into three parts, "Wives and Mothers,"
"Single and Working Women," and "Fallen Women," which
points out the "similarities and differences between
the position of women [in society] and the way it is
represented in the novel, that is to say the selection
used by the novelist." The purpose of the study is "to
get a better grip on the relationship of the creator
to his work and society. This attempt at 'demythifica-
tion' should help throw light on certain aspects of
Victorian values and culture."

    "The contemporary feminine ideal was that of Wife
and Mother. Her social position was one of subjection
and humiliation. The resulting tensions between ideal
and reality is one aspect of the problem of realism in
the Victorian novel." Such tension occurs in EG's own
marriage, where Mr. Gaskell kept his wife's literary
income despite their outwardly independent lives. In
her fiction EG drew female characters that both accorded
with and criticized the ideal conception of woman.
We find in LL a wife defying her husband's refusal to

permit her to find her wayward daughter. In RL the
wife convinces her husband to "resist blackmail" and
face social ostracism and poverty as a consequence.
In MB John Barton's wife had "saved" him from the iso-
lation and bitterness that urged his crime. In WD
Squire Hamely's invalid wife behaves angelically. And
Molly Gibson is moved to suffer unwelcome events in a
spirit of sacrifice and resignation. Margaret Hale
in NS must "repress all her personal worries" in
order to manage her family. She acts benevolently,
preventing Higgins from taking to alcohol and persuading
John Thornton to alter his views toward his workers.
She even gives her money to Thornton. "She embodies
the spirit of charity and philanthropy which . . . would
reconcile social classes and humanize the brutal world
of work." What more noble fate than this for a "potential wife-mother" than being responsible for this "almost
cosmic reconciliation" between disparities in English
life. Although EG worried little about the dependent
status of women--she does not portray a "middle-class
working wife" like herself--she could draw characters
in contrast to "the idealized wife-mother." The second
Mrs. Gibson in WD and Mrs. Thornton in NS are two such.

The depiction of single and working women must be
seen in light of the autonomy given the idea that a
woman's place is in the home. EG writes of the lives
of spinsters and working women more realistically than
her contemporaries; although, she too upholds the conventional attitudes of the time that the single life
was destructive and a poor alternative to married life.
Her spinsters have not married for family reasons.
Either class considerations bar a marriage, as in Miss
Matty's case in C, or economics plays a part: in MLL
Miss Galindo, an heiress, refuses a suitor because her
family believes him to be a fortune hunter. At times
sacrifices for family members prohibits a woman's
marrying: Deborah Jenkyns, Susan Dixon in HLA and
Ellinor in DNW are so bound. These spinsters are
socially active. Alice Wilson in MB, for example,
devotes her life to others. "This process seems to
be considered normal: once marriage has been ruled out
the only fulfilment for the aging single woman is to
devote herself to her neighbors, the poor, or her
family." But the personal price is high. Such lives
invariably induce and fix idiosyncratic behavior, foster
a nostalgia for a life denied them, breed sexual frustration and generate eccentric manifestations of the
maternal instinct. Although her spinsters lead "deprived" lives, morally EG was on their side, because
they usually worked and contributed something to society.
Idle women, like the second Mrs. Gibson in WD and

"Margaret Hale's cousins" in NS were inimical to EG.

In her portraits of working women EG pays little
attention to working conditions (except in NS) but
attempts rather to argue that working women expose
themselves to dangerous temptations, unfit themselves
for later married life and disrupt home life. "Mrs.
Gaskell's hostility to women working in factories had
humanitarian and moral motives. Her view corresponded
to that of Shaftesbury and the whole philanthropic
attitude which was founded on belief in the woman's
'nature'. All the same she did not support protective
legislation," which clearly would be "difficult to
maintain in Manchester."

On the subject of "the fallen woman" EG was "better
placed" than other writers "to tackle prostitution and
the tribulations of children." Esther's character in
MB shows how conventional was EG's attitude to such
people. "Esther remains the fallen woman of the moral-
ist." "Like the heroine of Lizzie Leigh, Esther loses
her child and is doomed to suffering and death." In
R, however, she treated the subject "with a new audacity."

In two earlier works, LL and MB, "while permitting
repentance and a return of lost innocence, she still
killed off the sinful woman and the child." In R she
holds "seducer, family and employer . . . responsible
for the tragedy." The "originality" in the novel is
in Ruth's relationship with Bellingham. Ruth's
refusal to marry Bellingham denies the presupposition
which more or less "underpinned" the conception of sinful
women and of females in general. With this refusal,
"which Jane Eyre did not dare make," EG has Ruth challenge
social conventions and assert her "moral superiority
over both the father of her child and over her judges."
"Bellingham's moral degradation parallels Ruth's spiritual
progression, this despite the very heavy punishment
inflicted on her by society. The inversion of generally
accepted notions in Bellingham's fall constitutes an
interesting variation on the double standard."

230   Easson, Angus. "Two Suppressed Opinions In Mrs.
       Gaskell's 'Life of Charlotte Brontë'," Brontë
       Society Transactions 11, 281-83.

The manuscript of LCB in the John Rylands University
Library of Manchester reveals EG's opinions of Emily
Brontë and CB that were omitted from the printed 1857
text. The first opinion has to do with Emily's stoical
death. EG, thinking of the impact of Emily's death

on Charlotte, wrote that Emily's conduct "was the very
essence of stern selfishness." The passage, scored
through, reveals "how ready Gaskell was to feel that
her judgment might be wrong or misleading." The second
opinion has to do with the deletion of a paragraph on
the subject of CB's attitude to Roman Catholicism.

231 Wheeler, Michael D. "The Writer as Reader in Mary
     Barton," Durham University Journal 67, 92-102.

     Examines EG's creative use of source material in
various incidents and in descriptions in MB. It is
shown that EG read and used, perhaps unconsciously,
material from "Caroline Bowles's Tales of the Factories
(1833), Thomas Carlyle's Sartor Resartus (1833-34),
Chartism (1839) and Past and Present (1843), Caroline
Norton's A Voice from the Factories (1836), 'The Dream'
(1840) and The Child of the Islands (1845), Charlotte
Elizabeth's The Wrongs of Woman (1843-44), and Elizabeth
Stone's William Langshawe (1842) and The Young Milliner
(1843)."

                           1975

232 Craik, Wendy Ann. Elizabeth Gaskell and the English
     Provincial Novel. London: Methuen & Co Ltd.
     "Bibliography," pp. 269-72.

     EG, the Brontë sisters, Anthony Trollope, George
Eliot and Thomas Hardy compose a group of authors who
are not "metropolitan" but "provincial" novelists.
They do not share the "culture and standards of London,"
rather they view London and its values as a "social
order" outside that which "the writer and his novel
inhabits." EG's five novels are examined to show her
development as an artist, how she develops from previous
writers and how much she is an innovator, and how she
stands in relation to these other provincial novelists.

     MB: This is a "new" form of novel written by a
"primitive" who seeks to "inform" not expressly "reform."
The novel suffers from "being an amalgam" of a tragic
story involving John Barton and a more conventional
plot involving Mary Barton, which shows that she only
partly achieved independence from the traditional form
of novel acceptable to the reading public. As evidenced
in this first novel, she accepts the Manchester world
as a "valid norm in itself," as opposed to London. She
does not write of Manchester from a position of "social
and geographical detachment," rather "her judgments rise

from and get their worth from her ability to participate,
at the same time she assesses. This stance in relation
to her setting and subject is the most obvious gift she
bestows on the nineteenth-century novelist--bestowed
in the way of most such gifts, so that the beneficiaries
are unaware of receiving it." Her realistic approach,
her introduction of original characters--John Barton
is "a victim of economic necessity and Mary Barton a
heroine put to a public test"--in the novel, her attention
to detail, her non-subordination of character, her
straight-forward speaking to her readers, and her psychological accuracy and brilliance in presenting the
reconciliation scene are all outstanding contributions
to the nineteenth-century novel.

R: This novel "shows a different and entirely
new subject, different areas of experience, a new range
of emotions, new kinds of characters, and a greatly
extended technique." The book is specially valuable
because it depicts Ruth's "progress of soul." This fact
makes necessary the plotting which brings Bellingham
back into the novel at the end. The story could have
been shortened, perhaps by excising scenes in which
Sally the Benson household servant appears.

NS: EG's "first major novel" because it handles
a wider range of material, it guides the reader's attention with greater deftness, is better proportioned
in handling character and action, shows her "perfect
ear for local speech," and with her heroine, Margaret
Hale, opens the way for characters like Dorothea Brook
and Romola. She never again creates a strong and
independent heroine like Margaret.

SL: "One of the greatest novels in the English
tongue." SL breaks ground by portraying the "tragic
greatness, and tragic ruin, of those who are humble
and obscured." The greatness of the novel springs,
in part, from her power to efface herself as narrator
and bring the reader into direct contact with the
experience of her characters. In SL her artistry is
supreme. In this novel she finds that she needs no
longer depend upon sensational action; in fact, she
subordinates action to her concern with "what happens
within people's minds and souls."

WD EG's "crowning achievement," characterized by
her having achieved a balanced state within herself,
reflected in the integration in the novel of all the
major themes from her other books. In this novel she
shows "interesting signs of change, a greater breadth
of understanding, and, where her relations with her

reader are concerned, total assurance."

233   Lansbury, Coral. Elizabeth Gaskell: The Novel of
        Social Crisis. London: Elek.

      Rev. by Mary Jacobus in TLS 14 Nov., 1352.

      (Not seen.)

234   Lansbury, Coral. "The Novels of Mrs Gaskell," TLS
        12 Dec., 1489.

      Letter in response to book review (see 233). "Ms
Jacobus is evidently pained that my work does not conform to male, capitalist, and Christian doctrine. I
am more distressed by her blinkered inability to compre-
hend anything that does not conform with the established
canon."

235   Nickel, Marjorie A. "The Dating of a Mrs. Gaskell
        Letter," N&Q NS 22 [218], 113.

      (Not seen.)

236   Rance, Nicholas. "Elizabeth Gaskell: Sylvia's Lovers
        (1863)," in The Historical Novel and Popular
        Politics in Nineteenth-century England. London:
        Vision Press, pp. 137-54. Vision Critical Studies,
        General Editor: Michael Egan.

      In SL EG does not write a historical novel divorced
from contemporary concerns. She attempts to analyze
"the birth of the Victorian middle-class sensibility,"
which had its origin in the 1790's. In writing of the
past EG does not intend to "isolate the past from the
reader, or to make him feel virtuous in comparison with
the rough old times." She sees backwards, moving
from the way things are in 1863 to their origins in
the 1790's. She treats "the earlier decade as the
vital prehistory of her own age."

      EG exposes the "myth of English stability," a
national trait denied to the French by English commen-
tators. She shows "that morals are socially conditioned
in the present, and must be influenced by political
change." The debate between Burke and Paine about the
rights of man are central to this analysis. Burke's
designation of the discontented lower classes as "the

mob" distorts the nature of the struggle in the 1790's
between classes. EG sides with Paine when she por-
trays the riot at the Randyvowse that results in the
freeing of pressed sailors and the hanging of Daniel
Robson. The presence of the press-gang in Monkshaven
is an imposition on the "open society" of the town. It
is an instrument of government, unjustly preying upon
English citizenry. "The novel shows no common interest
between the poor, who do the fighting, and the government
prosecuting the French war." The motive for the riot
is rational and justified even though events get out
of hand. The judges who hang Daniel Robson are equally
"mad" on their side. The press-gang is a "class instrument." "Dispassionately, Gaskell associates law with
the law-making society; and the law which backs the
press-gang also hangs Robson."

    EG, however, unlike Paine did not believe "free
enterprise a cure for the nation's evil." Rather, she
sees it as a force contributing to the establishing
of a middle-class, itself fearful of the working class
and willing to oppress it. Philip Hepburn's "fellow-
feeling is corroded by the new economic values." He
sides with the press-gang's activities in Monkshaven
and he abets the press-gang's abduction of Kinraid, his
rival for Sylvia. He earns money and rises commercially
in part because he is enterprising, in part because
he wishes to acquire Sylvia's love but in the process
he sets a value on Sylvia, as he would on a desirable
object. As he rises he becomes socially-conscious and
turns to religious activities to gain public recognition. "As religious energy is diverted to commerce
and used to gain wealth, so it permeates the pursuit
of Sylvia, who is to be 'shrined in the dearest sanc-
tuary of his being'; a discarded title for the novel
was 'Philip's Idol.'" By "putting a price-tag" on
Sylvia, Philip adopts "the values of the press-gang."

    Sylvia too is an in-between character. She is
drawn between her father's lower-class freedom from
self-consciousness and her mother's aspirations for
her to be a lady and marry the enterprising and respectable Philip. She compromises herself severely when
she marries Philip. She takes on the vanities of a
lady, even to the point of advocating that Philip,
back from the war and disfigured beyond recognition,
be driven out of Monkshaven, because he looks like a
vagrant.

    The Fosters serve EG's analysis of the rise of
"a new era" in the transaction of business. The Fosters
themselves are reluctant to disregard old ways of doing

business on trust. When they turn their shop over
to Philip and Coulson they retain control of the bank
they had been operating in conjunction with the shop.
"Here are the beginnings of that capitalist specialisa-
tion and concentration which in turn so disastrously
narrowed the lives of the workers." And it is significant that the Fosters are Quakers. Quaker virtues
of industry and honesty led, in the commercial world,
to wealth. They successfully applied "Puritan virtues"
to commerce. EG remarks of Jeremiah Foster that he
speaks with the same "peculiar tone" both when he
inventories the contents of his shop and when he reads
from the Bible.

Sylvia and Philip are reconciled by suffering and
by the truth in Philip's prophecy that Kinraid's heart
was fickle. Kinraid does marry when denied Sylvia.
But their reconciliation is based upon self-deception.
"Kinraid has married disillusioned with Sylvia's cal-
culating union, and wilfully adopting her criteria.
He aims for social and financial advantage, and his
wife is the doll that Hepburn tried to make of Sylvia,
a 'pretty, joyous, prosperous little bird of a woman'."

The latter part of the novel fails because the
characters are removed from the concrete world which
gave their thoughts and feelings some force. The child
of Philip and Sylvia's union, saved by Hepburn, goes
to America.

37 Sucksmith, Harvey Peter. "Mrs. Gaskell's Mary Barton
        and William Mudford's The Iron Shroud," Nineteenth
        Century Fiction 29, 460-63.

Citing the passage from MB (Knutsford ed. pp.194-95)
in which EG refers to a punishment about which she had
read, in which a man is crushed by the narrowing walls
of his cell, it is suggested that EG's source was The
Iron Shroud, a story published in Blackwood's Edinburgh
Magazine 28, 364. Mudford's story influenced Poe's
The Pit and the Pendulum (1843); however, since the
latter was not available in a "relevant collection of
Poe's stories," (Tales) until 1845, it seems likely
that EG's only source was Mudford's tale, and that she
read in the magazine not in a collection of Mudford's
stories. "If my conjectures are correct, Mrs. Gaskell
joins a growing company of early Victorian novelists,
including Dickens and the Brontës, who were impressed
and influenced by the fiction in Blackwood's."

APPENDIX I

EDITIONS OF THE WORKS

OF ELIZABETH GASKELL,

1929-1975

COLLECTED WORKS

238 The Works of Mrs. Gaskell. With Introductions by
A.W. Ward. London: John Murray, 1929. In Eight
Volumes. The Knutsford Edition. Reprint of The
Works of Mrs. Gaskell. Smith, Elder & Co., 1906.

239 The Works of Mrs. Gaskell. With Introductions by
A.W. Ward. New York: AMS Press, 1972. In Eight
Volumes. The Knutsford Edition. Reprint of The
Works of Mrs. Gaskell. New York: Putnam, 1906.

INDIVIDUAL WORKS

Mary Barton, A Tale of Manchester Life (1848)

240 Mary Barton. Introduction by Thomas Seccombe. London:
J.M. Dent & Sons Ltd; New York: E.P. Dutton & Co.,
Inc., 1932. Everyman's Library, no. 598. Reprinted
1961, 1965. (See 18.)

241 Mary Barton, A Tale of Manchester Life. London: Thomas
Nelson & Sons, 1934. Nelson's Classics.

242 Mary Barton. With an Introduction by Lettice Cooper.
London: John Lehmann Ltd, 1947. Chiltern Library,
no. 6. (See 61.)

243 Mary Barton. Introduction by Myron Brightfield. New
York: W.W. Norton & Co., Inc., 1958. The Norton
Library, no. 10. (See 107.)

244 Mary Barton, A Tale of Manchester Life. Introduction
by Kay Dick. London: Panther Books Ltd., 1966.
(See 158.)

245 Mary Barton, A Tale of Manchester Life. Introduction
        by Margaret Lane. London: J.M. Dent & Sons, Ltd;
        New York: E.P. Dutton & Co., Inc., 1967.
        Everyman's Library, no. 598. (See 173.)

246 Mary Barton, A Tale of Manchester Life. Edited, with
        an Introduction by Stephen Gill. Harmondsworth,
        England: Penguin Books Ltd, 1970. Penguin English
        Library. (See 197.)

                    Cranford. A Tale (1853)

247 Cranford. 8 Illus. by Miss Sybil Tawse. London: A. &
        C. Black Ltd, 1929.

248 Cranford. Preface by Anne Thackeray Ritchie. Illus.
        by Hugh Thomson. London: Macmillan & Co., Ltd.,
        1929. Reprinted 1935.

249 Cranford. London: Oxford University Press, 1929.
        World's Classics. Reprinted 1933.

250 Cranford. London: Macmillan & Co., Ltd., 1929.
        Cardinal Series.

251 Cranford. Illus. by A. Dixon. London: William Collins
        Sons & Co., Ltd., 1930. Canterbury Classics.

252 Cranford. Edited by Martin W. Sampson. New York: The
        Macmillan Company, 1930.

253 Cranford. London: William Collins Sons & Co., Ltd.,
        1931. Laurel and Gold Series.

254 Cranford. Illus. by Heber Thomson. London: Thomas
        Nelson & Sons, 1932. Nelson's Famous Books.
        Reprinted 1936.

255 Cranford. London: Thomas Nelson & Sons, 1933. Winchester
        Clasics.

256 Cranford, The Cage at Cranford, The Moorland Cottage.
        London, New York: Oxford University Press, 1934.
        World's Classics, no. 110. Reprinted 1935, 1944,
        1947, 1949, 1951. (See 314.)

257 Cranford. In Three Great Novels by Women Novelists:
        Pride and Prejudice Jane Austen, Jane Eyre
        Charlotte Brontë, Cranford Mrs. Gaskell. Illus.
        by A. Dixon. London: William Collins Sons &
        Co., Ltd., 1934.

258 Cranford. London: The Queensway Library, 1934.

                            110

259   <u>Cranford</u>. London: Oxford University Press, 1935.
         Hesperides Series. Limited to 500 copies.

260   <u>Cranford, a tale</u>. London, Glasgow: Collins Clear-type
         Press, 1937. Masterpieces of Literature, no. 57.

261   <u>Cranford</u>. London: William Collins Sons & Co., Ltd.,
         1937. Library of Classics.

262   "The Ladies of Cranford." A Play in two scenes
         dramatized from Mrs. Gaskell's <u>Cranford</u> by Edward
         Knoblock. London: Samuel French, Ltd., 1938.
         French's Acting Editions, no. 1702.

263   <u>Cranford</u>. Wood Engravings by Joan Hassall. London:
         George G. Harrap & Co., Ltd., 1940.

264   <u>Cranford</u>. London: Mellifont Press, 1946. Mellifont
         Classics, no. 20. Includes <u>Right at Last</u>, <u>The</u>
         <u>Manchester Marriage</u>, <u>The Crooked Branch</u>, <u>The Cage</u>
         <u>at Cranford</u>.

265   "A Cameo from Cranford." Adaptation from <u>Cranford</u> by
         Agnes Adam. New York: Universal Distributors;
         Glasgow: W. William McClellan, 1946. Northlight
         one act play series, ed. by Winifred Bannister.

266   <u>Cranford</u>. London: W. Foulsham & Co., Ltd., 1946.
         Foulsham's Boy and Girl Fiction Library. Reprinted
         with plates by B.F. Thorpe, 1948.

267   <u>Cranford</u> [and] <u>Cousin Phillis</u>. With an Introduction
         by Elizabeth Jenkins. London: John Lehmann Ltd,
         1947. Chiltern Library, no. 7. (See 63, 302.)

268   <u>Cranford</u>. Introduction by Robert Harding. London:
         P.R. Gawthorn Ltd, 1947. The Russell Classics
         Series. (See 62.)

269   <u>Cranford</u>. London: J.M. Dent & Sons, Ltd; New York:
         E.P. Dutton and Co., Inc., 1948. Everyman's
         Library, no. 83.

270   <u>Cranford</u>. Illus. by Arthur Wragg. London: C&J Temple,
         1947. Reprinted by Rockliff Pub. Corp.,
         1954.

271   <u>Cranford</u>. With exercises by J.C. Dent. London: Blackie
         and Son Ltd., 1948.

272   <u>Cranford</u>. With an Introduction by Angela Thirkell.
         Hamish Hamilton Ltd., 1951. Novel Library Series,
         no. 40. (See 83.)

273   "<u>Cranford</u>; a play in three acts adapted by Martyn

Coleman from the novel by Mrs. Gaskell." London:
Evans Brothers, Limited, 1952. Evans Plays Series,
ed. by Lionel Hale.

274 Cranford. With an Introduction by David Ascoli. London:
William Collins Sons & Co., 1952. (Actually pub.
Sept. 1953.) Collins New Classics Series, ed.
G.F. Maine, no. 540. Reprinted by W.W. Norton
& Co., Inc., 1959. (See 84.)

275 Cranford. London: Thomas Nelson & Sons, 1954.
Nelson's Classics. New ed.

276 Cranford. With an Introduction by Frank Swinnerton.
London: J.M. Dent & Sons Ltd; New York: E.P.
Dutton & Co., Inc., 1954. (Actually pub. Jan.
1955.) Everyman's Library, no. 83. Reprinted in
1964, 1966. (See 98.)

277 Cranford. London, New York, Toronto: W. Foulsham &
Co., Ltd., 1957.

278 "Cranford: A play from the novel by Mrs. Gaskell;
dramatized by Lorraine Plunkett." London: Blackie
& Son, Ltd, 1957. Troubadour Plays.

279 Cranford. With an Introduction and Notes by A.C. Ward.
London: Longman's, Green & Co., 1958. Heritage
of Literature Series, ed. by E.W. Parker--Section
B--no. 33 (See 114.)

280 Cranford. Simplified by E.M. Attwood. Illus. by
Wilfred Savage. London: Longman's, Green & Co.,
1958. Simplified English Series, ed. by C. Kingsley
Williams.

281 Cranford. London: University of London Press, 1966.
London English Literature Series.

282 Cranford. Retold by Beatrice Conway. London: Macmillan
& Co., Ltd, 1967. Stories to Remember Senior
Series.

283 Cranford. Freeport, L.I., New York: Books for Libraries,
Inc., 1971.

284 Cranford. Edited, with an Introduction by Elizabeth
Porges Watson. London: Oxford University Press,
1972. Oxford English Novels. Includes "The
Last Generation in England"(1849). (See 221.)

Ruth (1853)

285 Ruth. Introduction by Margaret Lane. London: J.M.

112

Dent & Sons Ltd; New York: E.P. Dutton & Co.,
Inc., 1967. Everyman's Library, no. 673. (See
174.)

North and South (1855)

286 North and South. With an Introduction by Elizabeth
Bowen. London: John Lehmann Ltd, 1951. (Actually
pub. Mar. 1952.) Chiltern Library, no. 21. (See
81.)

287 North and South. Introduction by Esther Alice Chadwick.
London: J.M. Dent & Sons Ltd; New York: E.P.
Dutton & Co., Inc., 1962. Everyman's Library,
no. 680. Reissue of edition first published in
1914. (See 125.)

288 North and South. Edited by Dorothy Collin. Introduction
by Martin Dodsworth. Harmondsworth, England:
Penguin Books Ltd., 1970. Penguin English Library.
(See 195.)

289 North and South. Edited, with an Introduction by Angus
Easson. London, New York: Oxford University
Press, 1973. Oxford English Novels. (See 223.)

The Life of Charlotte Brontë (1857)

290 The Life of Charlotte Brontë. Introduction by Clement
K. Shorter. London: Oxford University Press, 1939.
World's Classics, no. 214. Reprinted 1951, 1961.

291 The Life of Charlotte Brontë. Introduction by Margaret
Lane. London: John Lehmann Ltd, 1947. Chiltern
Library, no. 12. (See 64.)

292 The Life of Charlotte Brontë. Introduction by Margaret
Lane. New York: Duell, Sloan & Pearce, Inc;
Boston: Little, Brown & Co.; London: William
Heinemann, Ltd., 1953.

293 The Life of Charlotte Brontë. Introduction by May
Sinclair. London: J.M. Dent & Sons Ltd; E.P.
Dutton & Co., Inc., 1958. Everyman's Library,
no. 318. Reissue of edition first published in
1908. Reprinted in 1960. (See 113.)

294 The Life of Charlotte Brontë. New York: Doubleday, 1960.

295 The Life of Charlotte Brontë. Westport, Connecticut:
Greenwood Press, 1971.

296 The Life of Charlotte Brontë. Edited, with an Intro-
     duction by Winifred Gérin. London: Folio Society,
     1971.

297 The Life of Charlotte Brontë. With an Introduction
     and Notes by Clement K. Shorter. New York: AMS
     Press, 1973. Reprint of Harper & Publishers
     Publishers, 1900. Haworth Edition.

298 The Life of Charlotte Brontë. Reprint of the First
     Edition, Edited by Alan Shelston. Harmondsworth,
     England: Penguin Books Ltd., 1975. Penguin
     English Library.

Sylvia's Lovers (1863)

299 Sylvia's Lovers. Introduction by Arthur Pollard.
     London: J.M. Dent & Sons Ltd; New York: E.P
     Dutton & Co., Inc., 1964. Everyman's Library,
     no. 524. (See 139.)

Cousin Phillis (1864)

300 The Cage at Cranford, and Other Stories. Edited with
     an Introduction by Paul Beard. London: Thomas
     Nelson & Sons, 1937. Includes The Grey Woman,
     The Manchester Marriage, Half A Life-Time Ago,
     Cousin Phillis. (See 36, 315.)

301 Cousin Phillis; My Lady Ludlow; Half A Life-Time Ago;
     Right at Last. Introduction by Margaret Lane.
     London: J.M. Dent & Sons Ltd; New York: E.P.
     Dutton & Co., Inc., 1970. Everyman's Library,
     no. 615. (See 200.)

302 Cranford [and] Cousin Phillis. With an Introduction
     by Elizabeth Jenkins. London: John Lehmann
     Ltd, 1947. Chiltern Library, no. 7. (See 63,
     267.)

Wives and Daughters (1866)

303 Wives and Daughters. Adapted for easy reading by
     A. Sweaney. London: Oxford University Press,
     1937. Tales Retold For Easy Reading.

304 Wives and Daughters. Introduction by Rosamund Lehmann.
     London: John Lehmann Ltd, 1948. Chiltern Library,
     no. 18. (See 65.)

305 Wives and Daughters. Introduction by Margaret Lane.

London: J.M. Dent & Sons Ltd; New York: E.P.
Dutton & Co., Inc., 1966. Everyman's Library,
no. 110. (See 160.)

306   Wives and Daughters. Edited by Frank Glover Smith.
With an Introduction by Laurence Lerner.
Harmondsworth, England: Penguin Books Ltd., 1969.
Penguin English Library. (See 192.)

307   Wives and Daughters. London: Granada Publishing
Limited, 1971. Panther.

COLLECTED AND INDIVIDUAL
SHORT STORIES

Life in Manchester (1848)

308   Life in Manchester. Edited, with an Introduction by
J.A.V. Chapple. Manchester, England: The Lanca-
shire and Cheshire Antiquarian Society, 1968.
Includes Libbie Marsh's Three Eras, The Sexton's
Hero, Christmas Storms and Sunshine.

Lizzie Leigh, and Other Tales (1855)

309   Lizzie Leigh, and Other Tales. Freeport, L.I., New
York: Books for Libraries Press, 1972. Reprint
of Smith, Elder and Co., 1865 edition. Includes
Libbie Marsh's Three Eras, The Sexton's Hero,
Christmas Storms and Sunshine, Hand and Heart,
The Well of Pen-Morfa, The Heart of John Middleton,
Mr. Harrison's Confessions, Disappearances, Bessy's
Troubles at Home, The Old Nurse's Story, Morton
Hall, Traits and Stories of the Huguenots, My
French Master, The Squire's Story, Company Manners.

The Squire's Story (1855)

310   The Squire's Story. London: Todd Publishing Co., 1943.
Bantam Books.

311   The Squire's Story. London: Vallancy Press, 1944.

The Half-Brothers (1859)

312   The Half-Brothers. London: Gulliver Book Co., 1943.
Gulliver's Pocket Library: Famous Stories of All
Times, no. 17.

Lois the Witch (1859)

313   Lois the Witch. Illus. by Faith Jacques. London:

Methuen & Co., Ltd., 1960. Venture Library Series.

The Cage at Cranford (1863)

314 Cranford, The Cage at Cranford, The Moorland Cottage.
     London, New York: Oxford University Press, 1934.
     World's Classics, no. 110. Reprinted 1935, 1944,
     1947, 1949, 1951. (See 256.)

315 The Cage at Cranford, and Other Stories. Introduction
     by Paul Beard. London: Thomas Nelson & Sons,
     1937. Includes The Grey Woman, The Manchester
     Marriage, Half A Life-Time Ago, Cousin Phillis.
     (See 36, 300.)

APPENDIX II

A CHRONOLOGY OF

ELIZABETH GASKELL'S

LIFE AND WORKS

1810

29 Sept.   Elizabeth Cleghorn Stevenson born at 93 Lindsey
            Row (now Cheyne Walk), Chelsea, the second
            child of William and Elizabeth Holland Stevenson.

1811

Oct.   When her mother dies, Elizabeth goes to live
            with her Aunt Hannah Holland Lumb at Heathside,
            near Knutsford, Cheshire.

1825

            Elizabeth attends the Avonbank School at Stratford-
            on-Avon for two years, then returns to Heathside.

1827

            Her elder brother, John (b. 1799), disappears on
            a voyage to India. Elizabeth goes to stay with
            her ailing father and her stepmother in Chelsea.

1829

22 Mar.   Her father dies. Elizabeth moves to the home of
            the Reverend William Turner at Newcastle upon
            Tyne.

            She visits Edinburgh and Manchester.

1832

30 Aug.   Elizabeth marries William Gaskell (1805-84),
            assistant minister at Cross Street [Unitarian]

Chapel, Manchester, at the St. John The Baptist
Parish Church, Knutsford.

29 Sept.   After a honeymoon at Festiniog, Wales, the Gaskells
           settle, on Elizabeth's birthday, at 14 Dover
           Street, Manchester.

1833

Her first child, a daughter, is still-born.

1834

12 Sept.   Marianne Gaskell is born.

1835

10 Mar.-   Begins "My Diary: The Early Years of My Daughter
1838   Marianne." This work was privately printed
           by Clement King Shorter in 1923.

1836

Writes an early bit of verse, "On Visiting the
grave of my still-born little girl, Sunday
July 4th, 1836." This poem is published in
the "Introduction" to Mary Barton, vol. 1,
Knutsford Edition, 1906.

1837

Jan.   A poem "Sketches Among the Poor, No. 1," in
           Blackwood's Magazine.

5 Feb.   A daughter, Margaret Emily (Meta) Gaskell is born.

1 May   Aunt Hannah Lumb dies.

1840

"Clopton Hall," a short essay, included in William
Howitt's Visits to Remarkable Places.

1841

Mr. and Mrs. Gaskell make an extended journey on
the Continent, and while touring the Rhine
country meet for the first time William and

Mary Howitt.

1842

7 Oct.   Florence Elizabeth Gaskell is born.

The family moves to a larger dwelling at 121 Upper Rumford Street, Manchester.

1844

Autumn   William, her only son, is born.

1845

10 Aug.   William dies of scarlet fever in Wales.

1846

3 Sept.   Julia Bradford Gaskell is born.

1847

Publishes the following three stories in _Howitt's Journal_ under the pseudonym Cotton Mather Mills.

15 June   "Libbie Marsh's Three Eras."

28 Aug.   "The Sexton's Hero."

1848

1 Jan.   "Christmas Storms and Sunshine."

The stories are collected in the volume _Life in Manchester_ and published, still under pseudonym.

25 Oct.   _Mary Barton_ published in 2 vols. by Chapman and Hall.

1849

Spring   Meets literary figures such as Dickens, Thackeray, the Carlyles and John Forster during a London visit.

June   Meets Wordsworth at Ambleside.

July	"Hand and Heart" in The Sunday School Penny Magazine, and "The Last Generation in England" in Sartain's Union Magazine (New York and Philadelphia).
Dec.- Jan. 1850	The family moves to 42 Plymouth Grove, Manchester.

1850

30 Mar.- 13 Apr.	"Lizzie Leigh" in Household Words.
Summer	Meets Charles Eliot Norton in London.
June	"Martha Preston" in Sartain's Union Magazine (New York and Philadelphia).
19 Aug.	Meets Charlotte Brontë at Briery Close on Lake Windermere, home of the Kay-Shuttleworths.
16,23 Nov.	"The Well of Pen-Morfa" in Household Words.
Dec.	The Moorland Cottage published by Chapman and Hall (Christmas book).
28 Dec.	"The Heart of John Middleton" in Household Words.

1851

Feb.- Apr.	"Mr. Harrison's Confession" in The Ladies' Companion.
7 June	"Disappearances" in Household Words.
13 Dec.- May 1853	"Cranford" begun in Household Words.

1852

Jan.	"Bessy's Troubles at Home" in The Sunday School Penny Magazine.
April	Gives outline of Ruth to Charlotte Brontë.
19 June	"The Shah's English Gardner" in Household Words.
July- Aug.	On holiday at Silverdale.
Sept.	Dickens visits Elizabeth Gaskell at Plymouth Grove.
Dec.	"The Old Nurse's Story," in Household Words (Extra

Christmas Number).

1853

Jan.	<u>Ruth</u> published in 3 vols. by Chapman and Hall.
22 Jan.	"Cumberland Sheep-Shearers" in <u>Household Words</u>.
late April	Charlotte Brontë visits Elizabeth Gaskell at Plymouth Grove.
Spring	Harriet Beecher Stowe visits Elizabeth Gaskell at Plymouth Grove.
May	Serial publication of "Cranford" ends.
June	<u>Cranford</u> published by Chapman and Hall. Elizabeth Gaskell in London.
July-Aug.	Four eldest Gaskells go for a holiday in Normandy.
Sept.	Visits Charlotte Brontë at Haworth Parsonage.
22 Oct.	"Bran"(poem) in <u>Household Words</u>.
19,26 Nov.	"Morton Hall" in <u>Household Words</u>.
10 Dec.	"Traits and Stories of the Huguenots" in <u>Household Words</u>.
17,24 Dec.	"My French Master" in <u>Household Words</u>.
Dec.	"The Scholar's Story" and "The Squire's Story" in <u>Household Words</u> (Extra Christmas Number).

1854

25 Feb.	"Modern Greek Songs" in <u>Household Words</u>.
20 May	"Company Manners" in <u>Household Words</u>.
June	Charlotte Brontë marries the Reverend Arthur Nicholls.
2 Sept.-Jan. 1855	"North and South" begun in <u>Household Words</u>.

In this year Mr. Gaskell becomes senior minister of Cross Street Chapel, Manchester. Elizabeth Gaskell visits France with Marianne, where she meets Mme Mohl and William W. Story. She meets

Florence Nightingale in London. Last meeting with Charlotte Brontë.

1855

Jan.   "North and South" ends serial publication.

31 Mar.   Charlotte Brontë dies in Haworth Parsonage.

            Lizzie Leigh and Other Tales published by Chapman and Hall.

June   Requested by the Reverend Patrick Bronte to write The Life of Charlotte Brontë.

            North and South published in 2 vols. by Chapman and Hall.

25 Aug.   "An Accursed Race" in Household Words.

6-20 Oct.   "Half A Life-Time Ago," a revision of "Martha Preston"(1850), in Household Words.

1856

13-27 Dec. "The Poor Clare" in Household Words.

27 Dec.   "A Christmas Carol"(poem) in Household Words.

1857

13 Feb.-   Visits Paris and Rome with Marianne and Meta
May   and Catherine Winkworth.

Mar.   The Life of Charlotte Brontë published in 2 vols. by Smith, Elder & Co.

Mar.   Meets Charles Eliot Norton in Rome.

            "Introduction" to Mabel Vaughan by Miss Cummins published by Sampson, Low, Son & Co.

1858

Jan.   "The Doom of the Griffiths" in Harper's New Monthly Magazine(New York).

19 June-   "My Lady Ludlow" in Household Words.
25 Sept.

Autumn   Visits Heidelberg with Meta and Florence, then

122

Mme Mohl in Paris.

Nov.   "The Half-Brothers" in Dublin University Magazine.

27 Nov.   "The Sin of a Father" in Household Words. Renamed
              "Right at Last" in Right at Last and Other
              Tales (1860).

7 Dec.   "A Manchester Marriage" in Household Words
              (Christmas Number).

                          1859

              Round the Sofa and Other Tales published by
              Sampson, Low, Son & Co.

Summer   At Auchencairn, Scotland with her daughters.

8-22 Oct.   "Lois the Witch" in All the Year Round.

Nov.   Visits Whitby.

Dec.   "The Ghost in the Garden Room" in All the Year
              Round (Christmas Number). Renamed "The Crooked
              Branch" in Right at Last and Other Tales (1860).

                          1860

Feb.   "Curious if True" in Cornhill Magazine.

              Right at Last and Other Tales published by Sampson,
              Low, Son & Co.

July-   Visits Heidelberg with Meta and her friend.
Aug.

                          1861

5-19 Jan.   "The Grey Woman" in All the Year Round.

                          1862

Feb.-   Visits Paris, Normandy and Brittany with Meta and
May   a young friend.

May   "Six Weeks at Heppenheim" in Cornhill Magazine.

Oct.-   Exhausts herself in relief work for mill workers
Jan. 1863   of Manchester.

              "Introduction" to Garibaldi at Caprera by Colonel C.
              Augusto Vecchj published by Macmillan & Company.

                          123

24 Jan.-   "A Dark Night's Work" in <u>All</u> <u>the</u> <u>Year</u> <u>Round</u>.
21 Mar.

Feb.   In part to recuperate from physical exhaustion
              Elizabeth Gaskell visits Mme Mohl in Paris,
              then travels through the Italian hills to Rome.

21 Mar.   "An Italian Institution" in <u>All</u> <u>the</u> <u>Year</u> <u>Round</u>.

              A <u>Dark</u> <u>Night's</u> <u>Work</u> published by Smith, Elder
              & Co.

              <u>Sylvia's</u> <u>Lovers</u> published in 3 vols. by Smith
              Elder & Co.

8 Sept.   Florence marries Charles Crompton.

28 Nov.   "The Cage at Cranford" in <u>All</u> <u>the</u> <u>Year</u> <u>Round</u>.

Nov.-   "Cousin Phillis" in <u>Cornhill</u> <u>Magazine</u>.
Feb. 1864

Dec.   "Robert Gould Shaw" in <u>Macmillan's</u> <u>Magazine</u>.

Dec.   "How the First Floor Went to Crowley Castle"
              in <u>All</u> <u>the</u> <u>Year</u> <u>Round</u> (Christmas Number).

Feb.   "Cousin Phillis" ends serial publication.

Apr.-   "French Life" in <u>Fraser's</u> <u>Magazine</u>.
June

              Visits Pontresina.

Aug.-   "Wives and Daughters" in <u>Cornhill</u> <u>Magazine</u>.
Jan. 1866

              <u>Cousin</u> <u>Phillis</u> <u>and</u> <u>Other</u> <u>Tales</u> published by Smith,
              Elder & Co.

10 Mar.-   Visits Dieppe, then Mme Mohl in Paris.
April

              The <u>Grey</u> <u>Woman</u> <u>and</u> <u>Other</u> <u>Tales</u> published by Smith,
              Elder & Co.

              Purchases The Lawn, near Holybourne in Hampshire

for Mr. Gaskell.

2 Nov.   Elizabeth Gaskell dies at The Lawn.

6 Nov.   Buried at Brook Street [Unitarian] Chapel,
           Knutsford.

                            1866

an.   "Wives and Daughters" ends serial publication.

           Wives and Daughters published in 2 vols. by Smith,
           Elder & Co.

           ....

           Two fragments of Ghost Stories which Mrs. Gaskell
           wrote at some time in her life are printed in
           Cousin Phillis, vol. 7, The Knutsford Edition,
           1906.

INDEX OF AUTHORS

Chaloner, W.H. 112.

Chapman, Raymond 178.

Chapple, J.A.V. 156, 157,
166, 179, 182, 204, 308.

Chew, Samuel C. 20.

Clark, Alexander P. 108.

Colby, Robert A. 167.

Coleman, Martyn 273.

Collin, Dorothy 195,
208.

Collins, H.P. 90, 197.

Conway, Beatrice 282.

Coombes, H. 147, 155.

Cooper, Lettice 61, 242.

Cornell, Elizabeth 39.

Craik, Wendy Ann 232.

Cross, Wilbur L. 14.

Crow, John 38.

Cunliffe, John W. 24.

Curl, Joan 68.

Daniel, John 147, 155.

Delafield, E.M. 29.

Dent, J.C. 271.

Devonshire, Marion Gladys 2.

Dick, Kay 158, 244.

Dixon, A. 251, 257.

Dobbin, Andreena 165.

Dodsworth, Martin 133, 187,
195, 288.

Drabble, Margaret 147, 157.

Dumbreck, J.C. 112.

Dyson, Anne Jane 226.

Egan, Michael 236.

Easson, Angus 209, 223, 230,
289.

Eddy, Spencer L., Jr. 196.

Edwards, Olive 142.

Edwards, Tudor 143.

Eliot, T.S. 20.

Ellis, J.B. 168.

Esdaille, Arundell 99.

ffrench, Yvonne 20, 74, 109.

Fielding, K.J. 147, 157.

Ford, Boris 111.

Forster, E.M. 102.

Franko, Patricia 216.

Furbank, P.N. 224.

Ganz, Margaret 190, 228.

Gérin, Winifred 210, 196.

Gerould, Hordon Hall 45.

Gill, Stephen 197, 198, 246.

Goode, John 175.

Gorsky, Susan R. 225.

Gross, John 145, 147.

Grossman, L. 121.

INDEX OF ELIZABETH GASKELL TITLES

DATE DUE